FROM SELLING TO SERVING

THE ESSENCE OF CLIENT CREATION

LOU CASSARA

Dearborn™
Trade Publishing
A **Kaplan Professional** Company

This publication is designed to provide accurate and authoritative information in regard to the subject matter covered. It is sold with the understanding that the publisher is not engaged in rendering legal, accounting, or other professional service. If legal advice or other expert assistance is required, the services of a competent professional person should be sought.

Vice President and Publisher: Cynthia A. Zigmund
Acquisitions Editor: Mary B. Good
Senior Managing Editor: Jack Kiburz
Interior Design: Lucy Jenkins
Cover Design: Design Solutions
Typesetting: Elizabeth Pitts

Published by Dearborn Trade Publishing
A Kaplan Professional Company

Printed in the United States of America

04 05 06 10 9 8 7 6 5 4 3 2 1

Library of Congress Cataloging-in-Publication Data

Cassara, Lou.
    From selling to serving : the essence of client creation / Lou Cassara.
        p.   cm.
    Includes bibliographical references and index.
    ISBN 0-7931-9207-2 (6 × 9 hardcover)
    1. Customer relations. 2. Selling.   I. Title.
    HF5415.5.C38   2004
    658.8'12—dc22

                                                        2004001495

Dearborn Trade books are available at special quantity discounts to use for sales promotions, employee premiums, or educational purposes. Please call our Special Sales Department to order or for more information at 800-245-2665, e-mail trade@dearborn.com, or write to Dearborn Trade Publishing, 30 South Wacker Drive, Suite 2500, Chicago, IL 60606-7481.

Praise for *From Selling to Serving*

"I think you are going to love this book. It is full of insights, experiences, and advice that can transform your life and your business practices."
— Ken Blanchard, Coauthor, *The One Minute Manager*® and *The On-Time, On-Target Manager*

"A profound, refreshing book that only a person who walks the talk could have written. Lou has given us a classic that will inspire and challenge rookie and veteran alike. It is amazing that so much wisdom can be packed into so few pages."
— Charles "T" Jones, Author, *Life Is Tremendous*

"Lou Cassara is the best sales training coach I have ever worked with, bar none. Many of the concepts, tools, and applications he teaches through The Cassara Clinic have been incorporated into our professional development program that we encourage our best financial representatives to take."
— William H. Beckley, CLU, ChFC, MSFS, Executive Vice President–Agencies, Northwestern Mutual

"*From Selling to Serving* teaches individuals how to articulate who they are and the value they bring to society. Having served in the financial services industry for over 30 years and been involved in numerous excellent training and development programs, it is my opinion that this book can dramatically change your life."
— Earl J. Luttner, CLU, CEO and Chairman of the Board, Luttner Financial Group, Ltd., a Guardian Master General Agency

"This is the book face-to-face advisors and those dedicated to guiding them have been waiting for. Not since Ewing Carruthers wrote *A Way of Life* has anyone captured the essence of the mindset needed to connect the tactics, strategies, values, and vision necessary to create the framework for effective service to one's fellow man. Lou Cassara's passion flies off the pages!"
— Phillip C. Richards, CFP, CLU, RHU, CEO, North Star Resource Group, Immediate Past President, GAMA International

"Lou Cassara solves a fundamental problem in the financial services industry: how to teach advisors to become skillful cultivators

of productive client relationships. Knowing what other programs are now available in the industry, there is no question in my mind that within ten years The Cassara Clinic will be the industry standard."
— Dan Sullivan, President, The Strategic Coach

"An unfortunate historical problem in the industry has been 'too many amateurs teaching amateurs how to be amateurs.' So, it gives me great pleasure to have the opportunity to enthusiastically endorse Lou Cassara as a pro teaching pros how to be *even better* pros!"
— O. Alfred Granum, CLU, President, Granum Agency, Inc.

"Cassara's powerful message has the potential to permanently change your approach to selling and will help you rediscover the power of purpose in your work."
— Richard J. Leider, Founder, The Inventure Group, and Bestselling Author, *Repacking* and *Whistle While You Work*

"The concept of *From Selling to Serving* is not only an ethical process but also will best move the client from a 'felt' need to be comfortable to the 'real' need of finding purpose in his or her life and work."
— Colonel Nimrod "Mac" McNair, Director, The Executive Leadership Foundation

"Lou Cassara possesses a highly unusual combination of selling ability and talent, paired with an equally strong capacity to teach others how to serve clients. His insights are thought provoking, brilliant in their assessment of people, and articulate in helping others to see both the problems and the solutions in their lives. I consider *From Selling to Serving* a must-read for any sales professional."
— Robert H. Kerrigan, Jr., CLU, ChFC, Managing Partner, Strategic Financial Group, Strategic Benefits Group, a Member of the Northwestern Mutual Financial Network

"I have witnessed the impact Lou Cassara's programs have on financial services representatives. They acquire a new confidence and belief in their ability to truly make a difference. Lou's ideas

and concepts are transferable, and the results are measurable. I highly recommend his program for those who want to take their practices to the next level."
—Michael J. Vietri, Senior Vice President, MetLife

"Congratulations to Lou Cassara for being willing to tell the truth about the sales process. Selling has always been about relationships—not about products. In this book, Lou not only explains what is important, but he also gives you real tools to take back into the marketplace to build a more successful business. One career-changing concept is that of a 'personal value statement.' I'm sure most people have not even thought about this, and it is probably the most important concept any salesperson will ever use."
—Andy M. Schwartz, CFP, Northwestern Mutual Financial Network Top 20 All-Time Producer, Top of the Table Member, Million Dollar Roundtable

"Lou Cassara is one of the most important people in the financial products and services world. His book *From Selling To Service* is essential reading today for each person who is dedicated to serving clients and determined to vastly improve his or her own bottom line."
—Fred Kissling, Jr., CLU, MSPA, AEP, RFC, Publisher, *Financial Planning & Estate Quarterly, Leaders* Magazine, *Fraternal Monitor* Magazine, and *Probe* Newsletter

"*From Selling to Serving* promises to become the bible for financial planners, insurance agents, and other financial products and services advisors. This is the next best thing to attending The Cassara Clinic."
—Ed Morrow, CFP, CLU, ChFC, RFC, CEP, CEO, International Association of Registered Financial Consultants

"In *From Selling to Serving,* Lou Cassara shows how to bring more truth and authenticity into your client relationships. His unique client creation process reveals how to more effectively align your intentions with your actions."
—J. T. "Dock" Houk, JD, PhD, CPhD, CEO, National Heritage Foundation, World's Largest Group of Established Foundations

"Lou inspires readers to bring their life to their business and their business to life. For over 20 years, The Cassara Clinic has trained many of America's most successful financial planners, insurance agents, financial services advisors, entrepreneurs, and related professionals. This book offers most of the benefits of The Cassara Clinic, which is famous for producing superachievers in our industry!"

    —Louisa M. Montecalvo, CEP, CCPS, College Advisors Group, LLC

"From Selling to Serving offers readers the chance to grow in confidence, increase capability, gain clarity, excel in service, and vastly increase client numbers! Plus, there are even more benefits in these pages. Thank you, Louis J. Cassara."

    —Gayle M. Jendzejec, CLU, CFS, CEP, RFC, CCPS, College
        Advisors Group, LLC

"Lou Cassara's important work, *From Selling to Serving,* is certain to become a bestseller among books for financial advisors. This volume confirms the author's leadership position in our industry with his Cassara Clinic. No other title is, or has ever been, of such massive bottom-line benefit for readers who provide financial services."

    —Forrest Wallace Cato, Editor-in-Chief, *Financial Services Advisor*
        Magazine, and Author, *Napoleon Hill's Fast-Success Profile, What It*
        Takes to Make You GREAT, and *Become an Ambassador for Your*
        Specialty

"Few books for financial advisors are as valuable and useful as *From Selling* to *Serving.* Lou Cassara's title is possibly the most important book of this decade for members of our profession, because Lou paves the way for better serving far more clients."

    —William R. Lindsey, RFC, MSFS, AEP, Lindsey Financial Group,
        and Author, *The Wealthy Meat Cutter*

"Worth more than money itself! Actually, this volume means more money for every person who reads and applies Lou Cassara's valuable concepts."

    —Mark Matson, RFC, Author, *Lies Your Broker Told You,* and
        Manages Over $500 Million for Clients Worldwide

In loving memory of
Naomi Cassier and Alan Salus

You were and always will be the true
essence of service in my life.

Contents

PART ONE
THE ATTRACTION PRINCIPLE
You Are the Difference

PART TWO
THE CONNECTION PRINCIPLE
*Understanding and Activating
the Deep Emotions in Others*

PART THREE
THE COMMITMENT PRINCIPLE
Honoring Your Agreements

As I write these words, it is the Thanksgiving weekend and I have much to be thankful for. I am surrounded by the love of my family, my mom who is visiting, and my beautiful home. I just celebrated my 23rd wedding anniversary and 22 years in my career. I feel blessed in so many ways.

Many people have touched my life and made this book a reality. Some are still in my life, others have left or passed on. Some who I have never met touched me at the right time with the right words through their books. All have been teachers and shared their lessons and experiences. I am grateful to all these people for their knowledge and wisdom and for the impact they have had on my life:

- My wife, Debbie—for being my friend and always telling me the truth. You have been a consistent source of love and a model mother to our children.
- My children—Stefanie, Anthony, and Danielle—thank you for your love and support and all the great experiences that you allow me to share in your life. Go Boilers!
- My parents—especially my mom, Anna, who instilled in me through her actions the value of treating people with love and respect.
- My sister, Christine, and my brother, Chuck—thank you for being two of my biggest supporters.
- Tom Barbeau, my first sales manager—for believing in me and giving me a shot in sales without prior experience.
- Bob McGuffey—for bringing me into the life insurance industry and for going to bat for me time and time again.
- Al Granum, Bill Beckley, and John McTigue—my general agents. My special thanks to Al for all your guidance and mentoring during the early years of my career.

- Michelle Berry—thank you for "moving the piano," for all your hard work and dedication with getting The Cassara Clinic off the ground.
- To all the financial representatives, managing partners, and managing directors who have supported and participated in The Cassara Clinic and shared their experiences and knowledge—you have been the lifeblood of the program.
- My clients—thank you for the trust and confidence you place in me. It is an honor to serve you.
- My associates—it is truly a pleasure to be associated with a quality group of professionals like all of you.
- Craig Schaefer—for always being there when I needed someone to talk to and get a dose of reality.
- Ira Neiman—thank you for your support, for your friendship, and for being a resource of confidence and capability in my life.
- My friends and teachers—Mitch Anthony, Jim Autry, Wayne Dyer, David Hawkins, Louise Hay, Charlie Jones, Garry Kinder, Jack Kinder, Mac McNair, Jim Milonas, Maria Nemeth, Lance Secretan, Dan Sullivan, and Neale Donald Walsch—you have all stretched my mind with new ideas.
- To the people at Dearborn—especially Mary Good and Cynthia Zigmund for your patience with me and for believing in the project. My thanks to Jack Kiburz for fine-tuning my manuscript.
- Michelle Rathman—for the introduction to Dearborn.
- My team: Brian Strock—thank you for your extraordinary contribution and walking the path with me; Patty McKinley and Paula Hebert for holding down the fort and keeping things running while I focused on the book.

Above all—I thank God for the many blessings bestowed on me and for divinely guiding my life.

Lou Cassara
Burr Ridge, Illinois
November 30, 2003

I didn't know how to respond or what to think of the effusive and passionate (clearly Italian) voice on the phone telling me, "You are my soul brother. I read your book and said to myself, 'I could have written this. This is what I believe in.' We must find a way to work together, Mitch. For the good of this industry, we must find a way to collaborate and get this message out." This was my introduction to Lou Cassara—passionate and to the point.

Lou began to tell me about his Client Creator coaching program and about the impact it was making. *Great,* I thought, *here's another coach touting the merits of his coaching program.* After being approached by a score of coaches—some good, some decent, some weak—I had grown weary and leery of "the next great" coaching approach. But then I made two "tactical missteps": I agreed to meet Lou in person, and then I sat and watched him work.

After meeting Lou in person, I was deeply impressed with his own personal authenticity. He poured his heart out and showed me *why* he was instead of trying to impress me with *who* he was. He shared his vision of how the industry could become something better and something noble. He was ready to do whatever he had to do but admitted that he knew the job was too big for one or two people. He knew that it would take the alignment of many whose hearts were in the right place (the place of transformation) for this change to come to pass in financial services. I recognized the person before me was the real deal—not just in word but also in action and measurable results. I walked away shaking my head at Lou's level of commitment, determination, and, most important, his sincerity.

Then I sat in a room and watched Lou work with a group of Top of the Table veterans of 20 years. Lou taught them how to communicate the essence of who they were and the values and benefits they intended to bestow on their clients. It had nothing to do with selling their company or products; it had to do with selling the best part of who they were as human beings, how they could truly serve and add value. These highly successful financial professionals began to have individual epiphanies about how they were going to transcend their latest level of success. This group was cajoled and jolted by Lou Cassara into becoming authentic versions of themselves instead of boilerplate versions of what they thought their company might want them to be. They knew they had just found the key to making meaningful and lifetime connections, not only with their clients but also with the people who worked for them. I knew as I flew home that day that I had just witnessed the "tonic" for what ailed the financial services business.

Nothing is more common in the financial services industry than gurus promising to coach and motivate you and your business to the "next level." Some teach techniques, others offer strategies, and a vast number of so-called gurus produce very expensive vapor. Lou Cassara does something that seems to silence all the noisy hype and clutter—he helps take financial professionals to the next level of *being* and bring a profound level of authentic humanity to the business at hand.

Lou preaches that there should be no difference between who you are and what you do. I agree. The best work always has been done by those who have a sense of calling about their work. They don't leave their heart in the parking lot when they come to work. Lou has an unusual gift for helping individuals recognize the gifts and attributes they bring to the life of the client. More important, Lou teaches professionals how to articulate this authentically to clients.

There is no arguing with Lou Cassara. Not only is he a mesmerizing and passionate communicator, he is also a living, breathing, shining example of this ideology. He is a legend in the insurance business—one of the most successful in the history of the industry. People who have taken his instruction and coaching seminars immediately see increases in their work and life satisfaction and financial production. No coincidence there.

"The greatest gift you can give," Lou states, "is the example of your life working."

We all want our lives to work. We want to do well by doing good. We want to rise in value by adding value. Lou has developed a powerful process for making this happen in your life and business.

I am writing this Foreword to encourage you to let Lou Cassara into your life. Let Lou into your intellect and heart by reading this book. Let him into your business and life by participating in the inimitable Cassara Clinic coaching program. Let him into your organization by handing this book to people who can influence cultural change in your company.

Lou Cassara is not just another voice pointing to the future of this industry; he *is* a living, breathing model of that future.

—Mitch Anthony, author of *Your Clients for Life*, *The New Retirementality*, and *Selling with Emotional Intelligence*, and coauthor of *Storyselling for Financial Advisors* and *Making the Client Connection*

Leaders have a personal passion for making a difference, the ability to recognize when they are being called to serve and the courage to step forward and be seen taking action.

CHARLOTTE ROBERTS

WHEN IN DOUBT, TELL THE TRUTH

*"When in doubt, tell the truth.
It will gratify some of the people and astound the rest."*
MARK TWAIN

"The truth shall make you free."
JOHN 8:32

All progress begins by telling the truth. The truth is that people dislike being sold and love to be served. You know this intuitively and observe this truth every day. You know instinctively when someone is *selling you* or *serving you*. You recognize when you receive quality service and when you do not. What is the difference?

It all comes down to a feeling.

The essence of client creation is that people connect with and buy from people because they *feel* something, not because they *think* something. People buy on emotion and justify it with logic. The bottom line being communicated is *whose interest is being considered?* You feel *sold* when someone focuses on their best interest and *served* when the focus is on your best interest.

The truth is, we have all been at the giving and receiving end of both methods of communication. Both produce results—some very good and some very bad. Relationships are our primary teacher. The good ones reinforce what is working, and the bad ones provide the opportunity to make the necessary adjustments to better communicate and get along with others—that is, of course, if you are willing to pay attention and do so.

At the very least, your experiences raise questions:

- How do I find the balance between the two communication methods?

- How do I serve the needs of my clients while meeting obligations like paying my bills?
- How do I do things right for myself, and do the right things for others?

The truth is, you must do both. You must meet your felt needs for security and comfort while getting to your real need of feeling appreciated through your relationships. The essence of communication is seeing the world through someone else's perspective. Herein lies the challenge and the opportunity.

ATTENTION MUST BE PAID

The financial services industry is changing, and it is uncomfortable. There is a growing sense of anxious anticipation, apprehension, disenchantment, and betrayal in the workplace. Everywhere we look, there are studies and surveys showcasing a declining trend of ethics, values, and integrity in our society. The most prominent of these will be discussed throughout the book. The main issues they address are:

- 87 percent of clients that leave do so because of the relationship and not the company performance.
- 66 percent of current clients are considering changing advisors mainly due to unethical behavior.
- Only 35 percent of people in America today *feel* people can be trusted.

In his book, *Absolute Ethics: A Proven System for True Profitability,* Colonel Nimrod "Mac" McNair shares: "Our society tolerates a lack of integrity and even expects it." He addresses the fact that fewer and fewer professionals are operating from fixed values and keep changing them to fit the current circumstances. He describes this as *situation ethics*–or when all else fails, just lower your standards. This mindset of "if it feels good do it" is no longer effective and working. It is leaving people *feeling* tired and confused.

The proverbial question is, "What are we thinking?" Our best thinking got us here. Why are we so afraid to see our current reality and confront it? Most people are anxious to improve their circumstances but are unwilling to improve themselves. In the past 100 years, our technology has improved dramatically, but our ability to get along with each other has not improved much at all.

A DIFFERENT KIND OF HERO

The reason I am writing this book is because I appreciate and respect who you are and honor the work that you do. I have been blessed to be part of the sales and financial services industry since 1976, and I know the difference you make in people's lives every day. I realize the importance for you to have the opportunity to make a life for yourself and not just focus on making a living.

I genuinely care about our industry and would like to encourage you to bring your life to your business in order to bring your business to life—to share a process of successful achievement that will help you do what you do best and do it to the best of your ability. To recognize that the secret is: *Be who you are, it is all you need to be.*

This is a very important time for you. The challenges and chaos of change can provide you with great opportunities and a new beginning. There is more wealth and planning opportunities in our country than ever before, and more people are looking for financial guidance. You can provide a new leadership model to these people based on caring and supporting that can leave them *feeling* excited and inspired. The question before you is, What do you see, challenges or opportunities? How do you feel right now, confused or excited? Ask yourself the following: Am I tired or inspired at this time in my life?

Our society today is looking for a different kind of hero, a person who is ready and willing to get involved in their own life, answer the call to serve, and be seen taking action. This kind of hero is not the obvious hero we all relate to, such as a performer and athlete. This new hero will be admired for their courage and distinguished for action in the service of other people. This new kind of hero will have what I call an *authentic mindset*. They will be clear on who they are, confident in what they will do, and capable of knowing how they can serve others.

In addition, this person will define the word *hero* for today's society by:

- **H**onoring people. They are very clear that everything in their life depends on relationships and their ability to pay attention to them.
- **E**ncouraging people. They do not desire to be controlling bosses but prefer to build a community. They are not big on pep talks but in creating a place to share and do good work.
- **R**especting people. They do not limit, exploit, or manipulate people but love, care for, and inspire people to be all they are capable of.
- **O**pportunities for others. They do not hold onto everything but let go of their ego, which is the greatest barrier to leadership.

MY INTENTION

My intention for this book is to remind you: *Leadership is not what you do, it is what others do because you are there.* In my Client Creator process, you are your most important client. The journey of building to an authentic mindset and being a first-rate version of yourself begins with the pick-and-shovel work of self-reflection. You must understand it is *why* you do something that empowers you, not *how*.

In each of the three parts of this book, I will showcase the primary drivers of *clarity, confidence,* and *capability* that will allow you to *attract, connect,* and *commit* to significant client relationships. I will share with you the principles and patterns that create and sustain successful achievement, rather than simply ask you to imitate the actions of others. You will then develop an important understanding: *All relationships are a reflection of the relationship you have with yourself.*

In Part I, "The Attraction Principle," I will invite you to pay attention to the notion: *Who you are being is more important than what you are doing.* I'll ask you to be aware of why people are attracted to you and to know why people work with you. You will learn how to communicate your value clearly, effectively, and with purpose.

In Part II, "The Connection Principle," you will better understand how to activate deep emotions in others. You will develop an understanding that *your process of relating to others is your real product.* You will have the confidence and capability to connect to your clients' real needs.

In Part III, "The Commitment Principle," you will be reminded of *the value of honoring your agreements,* to understand the factors that influence decisions and why people commit. You will be more confident in converting obstacles to opportunities and helping yourself and others align intentions with actions.

Each chapter of this book will introduce a concept and provide a tool, where appropriate, to further your understanding. I also will provide specific applications and examples. Once you have finished reading and completed the exercises, you may want to revisit certain sections. In my workshops and professional coaching sessions, my clients are always interested in seeing the evolution of their answers over time. I encourage you to review and repeat the exercises to enhance your understanding of the three principles.

ARE YOU WILLING TO DO THIS?

One of the great gifts you give yourself is to be willing to do something. I will repeat this concept many times throughout this book. As a coach, I have never been able to help anyone make changes if they were unwilling to do so. You must be willing to look at something, see it for what it is, and tell the truth about it. *The toughest sale you will ever make is the one you must make to yourself.*

I have been in over 12,000 meetings in the past 20 years. My experience has been messy at times, and I have certainly made my share of mistakes. If you are willing to learn from my mistakes, I may be able to minimize yours. I have learned great lessons from certain experiences, and I will openly share them with you.

I also feel it is important to honor the old while embracing the new. Be loyal to what is working and leave behind what no longer serves you. Take what you can use and leave the rest. Your learning process is like mountain climbing—you use certain tools at certain levels and not before.

It has been my experience in my career that the better I *feel* about myself, the more effective I am in my life and work. Whenever I was in *pain,* it was because I had conflict between the truth I knew and the truth I lived. These moments can be your greatest teachers and provide new insights and understandings. At times like these in your life, it is not the time to do something as much as it is the time to know and be something.

It is my sincere intention that this book help you develop a new understanding—that a mindset of serving can change everything for you personally and professionally.

THE ATTRACTION PRINCIPLE

You Are the Difference

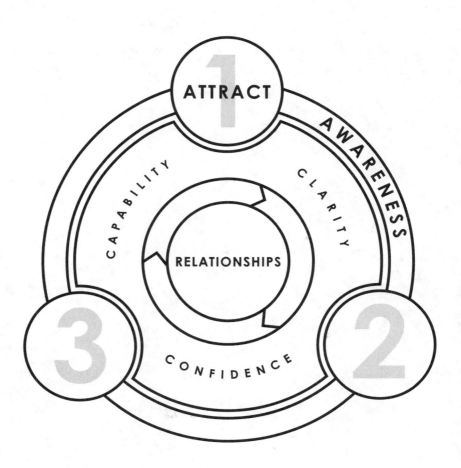

1

BE A FIRST-RATE VERSION
OF YOURSELF

"This above all: to thine own self be true."
WILLIAM SHAKESPEARE

"Insist on yourself; never imitate."
RALPH WALDO EMERSON

BUILDING TO AN AUTHENTIC MINDSET

Be **clear** *the key to your life and business is relationships.*

Be **confident** *it is easier for you to change yourself than to change others.*

Be **capable** *of understanding the principles and patterns that produce effective results.*

The key to your life and business is relationships. If you are willing to acknowledge this truth and develop an understanding that *all relationships are a reflection of the one you have with yourself,* it will change everything for you. It did for me.

To better understand your relationships, consider looking into yourself before you begin to connect with others around you. When you think about it, all relationships begin and are experienced in your mind, especially the relationship you have with yourself. If you don't think you're good enough, it's very difficult to make someone else think differently. The understanding that relationships are your primary teacher will help you to take the responsibility for your own actions and behaviors. People act as a mirror and reflect back to you exactly what you need to learn about yourself at any given time.

You will generally experience three levels of relationships. In the business world, the first level is superficial, simply addressing the features and benefits of a product or service. The second level is more sustaining and addresses the client's motives and values of why they would take action. The third level is your significant relationships, where you understand the client's emotional blueprint and core personality, which drive their behavior.

In gathering research for my own professional development, I conducted a survey in which I interviewed more than 200 successful entrepreneurs. I asked them specifically why they would or would not engage with certain professionals in financial services. My intention was to gain a better understanding of what their deciding factors were. The number-one reason they would not engage was that they felt they were being sold. It was most often put in these terms: "I got the feeling they were putting their interests ahead of mine."

The number-one reason they chose to work with someone was that they liked them and had a good feeling about them. The good feeling was about the individual, not the product or service. It became very clear to me that my first responsibility was to have people like who I was and for me to present a personality they could work with.

THE ESSENCE OF AN AUTHENTIC MINDSET

Think about the best relationships in your own life—personally and professionally. What is the one thing those relationships have in common? It is that both you and the other person appreciate each other for who you are. You don't have to pretend to be someone else around them. *You are being a first-rate version of yourself, rather than a second-rate version of someone else.*

We live in a culture that places little importance on self-reflection. My entry into sales and marketing was not a path chosen with much clarity or self-awareness. Like most of you, I was recruited and trained without a clear understanding of why I chose my career, what I would do, and how I would do it.

Without a clear understanding of these core questions, you can appreciate that confusion, rather than clarity, was the rule. Because of this, my growth strategy was to turn my will over to others, for them to tell me what to think and say and how to act. My empowerment strategy was simply to imitate the actions of those I viewed as "successful." This approach often resulted in added stress, conflict, and inconsistent levels of activity and performance. I felt inauthentic, adversarial, and uncertain. My head and heart were not in alignment. Finally, these feelings manifested in a career-changing experience.

I remember one sales manager very early in my career. Every day, he regaled us with his favorite techniques for manipulating a client and getting the check, even if it had "blood" all over it. I would smile and nod, while my stomach churned.

After one especially depressing session, I left to meet a potential client in downtown Chicago. He was a successful attorney, immaculately dressed and large enough to have played defensive end for the Chicago Bears. He also happened to be completely bald. His office was beautiful, and he sat in an overstuffed leather chair looking down at me. As I began to demonstrate my product, a dictation machine, I noticed that he was constantly looking over my head, as if something were going on behind me. After several minutes of this, I stopped my presentation and asked him, "Excuse me, sir, is something wrong?"

"Your hairpiece, where'd you get your hairpiece?" he asked.

"Sir, excuse me?" I stammered.

"Your hairpiece. Where did you get it?"

"It's not a hairpiece, sir. It's my hair. I'm just blessed with a good head of hair."

To my surprise, he totally ignored this and went on. "No, listen, I'm in the market for a hairpiece. Where'd you get it?"

I was perplexed. "Sir, honestly, this really is my hair."

He still didn't believe me and insisted I was wearing a hairpiece. Finally, he asked, "Can I touch it? I want to see what kind of quality it is."

I was already having a bad day, and now this man who wouldn't believe that my hair was real wanted to touch my head. I had never read or heard about how to overcome this kind of objection in any sales manual or training session. What was I supposed to do? When you are unclear on why you show up and what you have to offer, and all else fails, you tend toward the last resort: you lower your values.

"I'll tell you what," I said, "if I let you touch my hair, will you buy a machine?"

He paused for a second and then said, "OK."

So I stood up and leaned over his desk. He began to run his fingers through my hair, twisting and pulling and tugging for about 30 seconds. As I sat back down, looking a little like Don King, he said, "I can't believe that really is your hair."

As calmly as I could, I pulled out a sales order, placed it in front of him, and said, "If you'll endorse this, I'll have your machine delivered to you tomorrow." Without even hesitating, he signed the order.

I left the meeting with mixed emotions, not really sure what to take away from the experience. I arrived back at the office, only to be pounced upon by my sales manager. "Well, did you get the order? Did you do what I told you to do?"

"Yeah, I got it, but I didn't do what you told me to do. I used the 'Lou-do' close."

It was at this point I realized that trying to imitate the success of others was a dead end. The prevailing adversarial model of the day may have worked for some (though I doubt for long), but it definitely wasn't going to work for me—and I certainly wasn't about to start using the Lou-do close on others. I began to understand, however, that the only way for me to succeed was to stop trying to be like someone else and start developing my own unique value as a professional. Being a John Wayne fan when I was a kid, it was time to apply a little cowboy wisdom in my life: *When your horse dies, get off.*

WHEN THE PRO IS READY, THE CLIENT WILL APPEAR

This experience led me to begin the discovery process to better understand how to create significant relationships, starting with myself. The opportunity before me was to have the courage to see my current reality and confront it, to choose to acknowledge that some of my beliefs about relationships were no longer effective and working. I sought to have a better understanding of why I acted the way I did and, for the most part, why I was not using my talents and abilities in a consistent manner. I was beginning to learn a very important life lesson.

Most people are anxious to improve their circumstances but unwilling to improve themselves. They are either reluctant to do the inner work of self-reflection or simply don't know how. However, consider this: *It is easier to change yourself than it is to change others.* When you realize this simple truth, you will begin to understand the importance of uncovering and understanding your authentic self.

The problem is that we are not taught *how* to learn. Most training focuses on product knowledge and company information, which, although important, has nothing to do with how to relate and communicate with others. Learning the sales process involves memorization of standardized scripts that are not related to the individual's values, unique abilities, or experience. We are taught *how* to do something before fully understanding *why* we would do it.

As a sales coach, I have worked with and studied people's behavior for the past 18 years. I have observed that people who create and sustain sales success over a long period of time, understand and operate from certain patterns that produce effective results. These patterns, or *drivers,* I have identified as clarity, confidence, and capability, and these people are *being:*

- *Clear* about who they are.
- *Confident* in what they will and will not do.
- *Capable* of aligning their intentions with actions.

They have experienced what I call an authentic mindset, or a state of mind that allows them to maximize their performance. They embrace and operate from powerful attractor patterns that produce success, not just imitate the actions of others. They are clear on their intentions, who they are, and what values and qualities they can share. They are confident about how they can serve and what actions they deliver. They are capable of honoring their agreements and keeping their promises, and, above all, they are committed to the necessary effort to produce the desired result.

You most likely know someone who has this Midas touch; no matter what they do, they do it well. You can take everything away from this person, move them to another location, and, in a very short period of time, they will re-create their success. Authentic people know that they *are* the difference.

I will emphasize clarity, confidence, and capability throughout the book. The understanding of these drivers will increase your state of readiness and allow you to go to another level in your client relationships. They are fundamental to building an authentic mindset, which will allow you to attract, connect, and commit to significant client relationships.

Clarity: To be certain, open, and direct about something.

Confidence: The ability to think clearly, communicate effectively, and take authentic action.

Capability: The result of combining your knowledge, talents, and skills to organize ideas and align intentions with actions.

THE VENDING MACHINE THEORY

People imitate techniques of others as if they were candy in a vending machine. They pull on the knob of the technique that fills the need, much like choosing candy to fill a sweet tooth, and out comes someone else's process. The "goodies" are dispensed, and you hope that it works. You try it for 30 days, and if you don't like it, you can try something else. However, pulling the knob and trying someone else's process will give you superficial results. The "results" dispensed will vanish as fast as a sugar high.

How many times have you tried to copy the actions of someone in your office? Even when you say what others say, and act as others do, the understanding behind the process is missing. Results may follow, but the actions of imitation will not sustain without the clarity of understanding why they came about. *To be truly successful, it is necessary to operate from principles that produce success, not just to imitate the actions of others.*

In a coaching session, Tom B., a financial representative, told me he spent the first ten years of his life insurance career trying to be Al Granum, because he was told that was the only way to succeed in the business. While that method has worked for countless other people, it did not work for Tom at all. He said, "I am a really bad imitation of Al Granum." He felt a bit foolish, admitting that as a 50-year-old man he needed someone else's permission to run his business the way he thought it should be run. I shared with him the benefits of being a first-rate version of himself, and how that could make his process more authentic. After our session, he felt more courageous to use his own unique process without feeling guilty. Using his own natural style, he was able to double his annual income and then double it again the following year.

Being clear about who you are, what you will do, and how you will do it will dramatically affect your ability to attract, connect with, and commit to significant relationships.

BENEFITS OF BEING AUTHENTIC

In their book *Soar with Your Strengths* (Delacorte,1992), authors Donald Clifton and Paula Nelson suggest that if you focus on what you like best and do it to the best of your ability, you will not only be authentic, you also will be building on your strengths and, therefore, realize more of your potential than if you were trying to improve on your weaknesses. As you nurture your strengths, you will gain confidence. When you are coming from a place of integrity and utilizing your unique gifts as a person, you will have a much different experience meeting with a prospective client. Your delivery will be natural, and your communication more effective. Tell your own truth.

It all starts with authenticity. Take an example from the retail sector. Sam Walton, Wal-Mart's founder, understood the leading pattern that attracted clients: service. To honor that in his discount stores, he installed greeters at the doors armed with the understanding that, no matter what, a shopper's needs came first. The importance of service was a part of who Sam Walton was, and it was reflected in his stores.

In the mid-1980s, upstart Venture saw the success of Wal-Mart and tried to copy that model in its own stores. What happened? A big problem arose because Venture, along with its customers, was unclear on who it was and what it was trying to be. They wanted to emulate the success of Wal-Mart, but they didn't understand the special feeling of service that Wal-Mart gave its shoppers. The retailer was being a second-rate version of Wal-Mart instead of a first-rate version of Venture. It lacked a clear understanding of *why* Wal-Mart was so successful. Although many other factors were involved as well, the company went out of business within a few years.

We see examples of this lack of clarity every day, and we recognize it immediately. The attempt to mimic others is transparent and inauthentic. If Venture had done the hard work of introspection—discovering its unique value—it could have built its business from something real, something authentic. Certainly, shoppers would have responded.

On the other hand, the popular chain Target rose to prominence at the same time as Venture's decline. Although Target carries products similar to Wal-Mart and uses a similar low-price strategy, both stores survive and even thrive, sometimes within blocks of one another. Target is a direct competitor with Wal-Mart. What did they do that Venture failed to do? They communicate clearly to their shoppers who they are. Their confidence in what they will do and consistent capability to follow through with their clients stem from this clarity. Each store—Target and Wal-Mart—appeals to a distinct type of price-sensitive consumer, based on the authentic personality each embodies.

Here's an important understanding: *You know what you need to know.* You have a unique gift that no one else has. Your journey is to identify it and do it to the very best of your ability.

WHY would you consider being authentic?	HOW will you do it?
To be **W**hole	By being **H**onest
To be **H**appy	By being **O**pen-minded
To be **Y**ourself	By being **W**illing

To be Whole: To align your thoughts, words, and deeds

To be Happy: To be content with who you are

To be Yourself: To express your unique abilities

The authentic mindset consistently reinforces your own beliefs and values. *Be who you are; it is all you need to be.* Authenticity is where your real power comes from. It is what allows you to be a person of impact.

I recognized that my purpose in life is not my job description. One of the ways I experience my authenticity is through a career that allows me to express myself. My experience taught me that my success or failure was in direct proportion to my ability to reflect on the following questions, questions only I could answer for myself. The exercise that follows is designed to help you identify your unique value as a person and establish a vision for yourself, with questions derived from the three drivers, *clarity, confidence,* and *capability.* Think about your answers to these questions and write your responses on the pages of this book or on a separate sheet. Each person will fill these out differently, and there are no wrong answers. Once you have progressed further into this book, you may find that you need to refine or revise your answers.

The questions are simple, but they are not necessarily easy. They are questions only you can answer and likely have not been asked before in relation to your career. In this exercise, I have filled out my responses to each question as an example. This is meant to help you think about the questions but obviously cannot substitute for your own thoughts. Above all, the questions require reflection and introspection.

A*u t h e n t i c* **T***r u t h s*

- All relationships are a reflection of the one you have with yourself.

- To be truly successful, it is necessary to operate from principles that produce success, not just to imitate the actions of others.

- Be who you are; it is all you need to be.

BUILDING TO AN AUTHENTIC MINDSET

EXERCISE

Why am I here? (Why do I get up in the morning?)

What will I do? (What is the best way I can serve others?)

How will I do it? (What roles demonstrate how can I serve others?)

BUILDING TO AN AUTHENTIC MINDSET

EXERCISE

Why am I here? (Why do I get up in the morning?)

For the purpose of being a resource of clarity and confidence to others.
To guide people and businesses to realize their true potential.

What will I do? (What is the best way I can serve others?)

To encourage people to do what they do best and do it to the best of their ability.

How will I do it? (What roles demonstrate how can I serve others?)

To lead and serve others through my teaching, speaking, and writing.

2

THE ESSENCE OF ATTRACTION

"To be nobody but yourself in a world which is doing its best to make you everybody else—means to fight the hardest battle which any human being can fight and never stop fighting."
E.E. CUMMINGS

"If you want a quality, act as if you already had it."
WILLIAM JAMES

BUILDING TO AN AUTHENTIC MINDSET

Be **clear** who you are, is more important than what you do.

Be **confident** your external effort will be driven by your core beliefs.

Be **capable** of paying attention to what you are thinking at any given time.

We see the essence of attraction at work every day. Think of two people in your profession with relatively equal skills and abilities. Both graduated from college, both understand the nature of what they are doing, both have similar intelligence, and both are provided with similar resources. Yet, one person is earning a great income, while the other barely gets by—and they're both doing the same thing. What makes the difference?

WHO YOU ARE IS MORE IMPORTANT THAN WHAT YOU DO

The difference is all in one's clarity of understanding about attractor patterns. One is successful and the other is not, not because of anything either is doing but because of what both are *being*. The successful professional is being clear on why they show up every day. They attract prospects and clients because they are being open, friendly, caring, helpful, and considerate with people. They are being confident that their work matters and that it amounts to something more than themselves. They are capable of using their talents and abilities and of the necessary effort to produce great results.

The other professional is *not* being clear about why they show up. They lack the confidence in what they say and how they act. In many cases, they are being close-minded, distant, uncaring, inconsiderate, and even resentful in what they are doing. I observe scenarios like this all the time. Those who are willing to build an authentic mindset and successfully attract others *pay attention to what is going on inside of them in any given moment.* They connect with the fact that they are human beings, not human *doings*. What they do is a direct result of who they are being. Pay attention to this very important truth. It can radically transform your effectiveness with your relationships.

The essence of attraction: Paying attention to what is going on inside of you at any given moment.

Years ago, I was researching doctors to perform my hip-replacement surgery. Not a subject I took lightly at all, I narrowed down my field of prospects to the top two surgeons in the Chicago area and made appointments to interview them.

I arrived at the first doctor's office on time. The doctor, I'll call him Dr. G., was well known in his field. Judging from the number of placards, medical journal clippings, and diplomas on the waiting room walls, he had enjoyed a very successful career (and wanted his patients to know it). I was coldly greeted by the receptionist, as she shoved a clipboard at me and told me to sign in. I then waited for another ten minutes before I was given a stack of forms to fill out while I waited to be called. The forms were confusing—I knew why I was there and what kind of information I was seeking, but the forms didn't seem to match any of that. The receptionist must have been busy, because she had no time to answer my questions, nor would she give me any idea when I would be called.

Nearly a half hour and three back issues of *Time* later, I was ushered into an examining room. When the doctor and his intern finally banged open the door to the exam room, Dr. G. didn't even bother to introduce himself or glance my way. He looked at my X-rays and at the stack of forms I had completed, while I just sat there. He then announced to his intern, "This person doesn't need surgery," and walked out of the room. His intern stayed behind to ask me many of the routine questions I had already answered on the forms. I remained in the office only long enough to say I wasn't interested in going any further in their process. At that point, I mirrored back to the intern exactly how the doctor treated me. I felt no connection, I disengaged, and I left.

My experience with the second surgeon, Dr. H., was entirely different. Both doctors had similar backgrounds—well respected by their peers, renowned for their surgical prowess—but Dr. H. had something more. The receptionist greeted me professionally and politely as soon as I walked into the waiting room. I was given a short form to fill out, and I was quickly escorted to the exam room by the nurse. Within minutes, Dr. H. knocked on the door and entered with my paperwork and X-rays in hand. He introduced himself and sat down, and I assumed he would look over my X-rays as the first doctor did. Instead, he offered me his hand. "Hello, Lou," he said. "How are you feeling?"

"Have you reviewed my X-rays?" I asked.

"I don't operate on X-rays," he said to me with a gentle tone. "I operate on people. How do you feel right now?"

I made my decision right there and then. I had experienced the working persona of each doctor, and I immediately felt a connection to Dr. H. Yes, his office provided better client service than that of his colleague, but my decision was based on the genuine attitude of Dr. H. He was able to attract me as a patient, because he made me *feel* that my best interest was being served. He treated me as a person, rather than a nonentity. In essence, who he was *being* was more important than what he was *doing*.

A NEW UNDERSTANDING:
BE-DO-HAVE VERSUS HAVE-DO-BE

We've been raised in the old understanding that people want to *have* something so they decide to *do* something and consequently can *be* someone. For example, think of when you began your career. When you started, you were told that if you wanted to *have* something (such as success), you should go *do* something (such as work 80 hours a week), so you could *be* happy. In this external mindset, you operate in order to achieve something outside of your control. While someday you may be successful, this paradigm keeps cycling. You will keep wanting more—increasing the amount of things you need to reach personal "happiness." The end result is the feeling of obligation to do more. The outcome is ultimately elusive: the "do, do, do" cycle will prevent you from ever feeling satisfied, leaving you tired and confused.

The most basic actions we *do* in our lives are done so that we can *be* something. We do this thing called eating so we can be nourished. We do this thing called sleeping so we can be rested. We do this thing called talking so we can be understood. At the end of the day, everything we do in our lives is for the purpose of being something.

People who create and sustain successful achievement start from the place of being something first. The person who chooses to have abundance in their life understands that it is important to be a resource of that for another person. For example, the quickest way you can have abundance in your life is be a resource of abundance for another person. *Whatever you choose to have for yourself, be the resource of that for another.* Successful people know this and live by this very important understanding. This understanding can be applied by anyone. You do not have to default to a label to define who you are and what you do. If you do, you allow the other person to determine the perceived value and whether they are interested.

Art the shoeshine man provided an example of this. I met Art as I was passing through a hotel lobby on my way to lead a workshop. He caught my eye and immediately asked in a friendly manner, "Shoeshine, young man?" I felt I didn't need a shine and replied with the usual, "No thanks." Instead of giving up, Art gave me a reason to consider his service. "You know," he said, "I help people make big deals with shiny heels." Although I felt I didn't need a shoeshine, I was attracted to his statement and courageous attitude. I chose to sit in his chair and talk to him while I had my shoes shined. I really connected with his approach and style. He made me feel very comfortable in his presence.

Art understood intuitively that people are looking for a reason to connect. He attracted me, because he was able to tap into what I regarded as valuable. He was being cordial and outgoing. He had the ability to provide more than a mere service to others, and he let me know it. I was attracted to his statement, because he expressed a value in his work. He did not look at himself as "just a shoeshine man," defining himself with a label. He presented himself as a unique resource and, by doing so, attracted me to his service. The real benefit to Art was that I later introduced him to all the people in my workshop, and he had the pleasant result of more business than he could handle.

HOW DO YOU BE-HAVE?

The ability to attract is to know what people connect with. People connect with attractor patterns such as authenticity, clarity, confidence, service, and kindness. Those with a service mindset are able to live that connection through their actions. In essence, they are *be-having*. I define behavior as *having the experience of who you are being*. Break the word apart. *Be* something first, and then *have* it. *Be* starts it all, and the rest follows naturally. Show me a person who is kind, considerate, and compassionate to others, and I will show you a person who has more clients and friends than they can handle.

> **Behavior:** Having the experience of who you are being.

With this understanding, let me ask you a question. Would you rather *be* financially independent or *have* financial security? To be financially independent represents a state of mind, grounded in the understanding of how to reach financial independence. Having financial independence suggests you could lose it. Your understanding of money is not grounded in the principles and patterns that produced the wealth in the first place.

It is much harder to maintain something than to obtain it. Lottery winners experience this on a regular basis. Because they are handed the money without the understanding of how to create and sustain it, they become dependent on others to show them how to keep it. You oftentimes hear stories of lottery winners who lose their winnings within a short time, because they never learned this important pattern of behavior. For many, they are being unconscious about how money works, doing frivolous spending, and ultimately have the least desired results—loss—the very thing they did not want.

I will also share another important secret: *Your external effort in your career will be in direct proportion to your internal conviction.* So, pay close attention to these beliefs and thoughts. They will guide your behavior and actions. You will produce exactly what you are thinking at any given time. For me, an authentic mindset was the bridge between the external and internal beliefs that I had. The transition I was seeking was to be effective in my craft while being authentic, transparent, and truthful along the way with other people.

BEHAVIOR: FROM THE EXTERNAL TO THE INTERNAL

Before you can connect with the authentic mindset model, you will have to examine and understand your core beliefs. This is vitally important, because you cannot change an action without identifying and understanding the underlying belief that supports it. For example, I have mentioned earlier if you do not believe you are good enough, which is the most common belief I observe in professional salespeople, it is very difficult to change your actions and behavior.

This is one of the problems with typical sales training. We are typically inundated with information but do not take time to reflect or pay attention to the beliefs we have regarding the critical components of a selling profession. Problems arise for many due to a lack of clarity on the following elements:

- A personal view of selling
- Understanding of abilities
- Commitment to activity
- Belief in product
- Personal values

As a sales coach, I have consistently observed that the lack of understanding of the core beliefs on these elements actually creates conflict, stress, and low activity. This is mainly due to the fact that training does not align these elements, and professionals oftentimes appear inauthentic, competitive, and uncertain. It is also important to note that initial training does not ordinarily address these issues, and it would be important for you to develop these on your own.

I have been in countless coaching sessions where the professional appears to be in a slump. After the drilling down and digging deeper into the reasons, I often hear that their family is not supporting their current career choice. There have been many life insurance professionals who have had negative feedback from their family with regard to their choice of career. Their parents are "disappointed" that having invested a significant amount in a college education their children then go sell life insurance. The beliefs created by others have a deep impact on these professionals' performance.

This is especially true with your belief in your own product or service. I have observed many times professionals attempting to offer a solution without actually purchasing or utilizing it themselves. How can they possibly be effective or have integrity without being able to demonstrate that they personally have made the investment or commitment? A prospect or client can easily knock you off center by simply asking you about your own experience with the solution you are proposing.

For example, I was recently in a meeting where the CPA was engaged in a discussion with a client and myself about a buy-sell agreement. I was explaining the various types of agreements the client could consider with his partner and shared my own experience with my partner. At that point, the client asked the CPA for his input on what he had done with the partners in his firm. The CPA jokingly responded that he should listen to me, because he had not gotten around to doing his yet. The client was unimpressed with the CPA's response and later told me so. He was irritated with the fact that he was being charged for the CPA's time, and he could not add value to the discussion.

By far, the most important belief to understand about yourself is how you feel about money. Money itself is neutral, but, as you know, it is packed with emotions and energy around how it is used in our lives. So many people have a very difficult time dealing with this issue, especially with the belief that there is never enough money to make ends meet. Deep down, financial disasters are created due to a core belief that you are not worthy of having money.

Think of the language used to express money. It is based on deep, core values that are extremely emotional. Look at how similar the language is that we use to describe relationships: bonds, shares, trusts, maturity, appreciation, securities, and net worth. Currency bills themselves are called tender. My experience has taught me that I cannot talk to clients about their money without talking about their life.

I will not attempt to go into this subject in great detail. I simply want you to address your core beliefs, as they will dramatically affect your business performance. If your career is in a mode of fits and starts, highs and lows, and appears to be an emotional roller coaster, examine your beliefs. So many times, it boils down to the feeling that you are not good enough. *I'm here to tell you that you are.* A way to help you examine your core beliefs and move from the external is to ask yourself how you feel about the answers to the following questions:

- Is your purpose to make money or make a difference?
- Is your intention to sell someone or to serve them?
- Do you view your work as an obligation or an opportunity?
- Are your agreements with people limiting, exploiting, and manipulating, or truthful, transparent, and authentic?
- Are you competitive and adversarial or supportive and collaborative in your relationships?

I want to emphasize that there are no wrong answers to these questions. Simply be aware of your core beliefs, and how you currently engage people. From my own experience, I recognize without a complete understanding of these core beliefs, what I was projecting to other people was in many cases the direct opposite of how I perceived myself communicating with them.

THE LAW OF ATTRACTION

The law of attraction: You will attract the very people and circumstances you need at any given time.

The Be-Do-Have understanding is powerful. While your answers to these three short questions may feel obvious to you, it's important to write them down and think about what they mean. Start from the *being,* and the behavior and results are possible. As in the previous chapter, I've included my own answers as a guide.

A *u t h e n t i c* T *r u t h s*

- Who you are being is more important than what you are doing.

- Whatever you choose to have for yourself, the best way to obtain it is to be a resource of it for another.

- The external effort that you are willing to make is in direct proportion to the internal conviction you have.

THE EXTERNAL VERSUS THE INTERNAL		
External (Have-Do-Be)	**The Authentic Mindset**	**Internal** (Be-Do-Have)
Make Money	*Purpose*	Make a Difference
Limit Exploit Manipulate	*Intentions*	Authentic Transparent Truthful
Obligation	*Motivation*	Opportunity
To Sell	*Agreement*	To Serve
Competitive/Adversarial	*Communication*	Collaborate/Supportive
Leaves you:		Leaves you:
• Doing More		• Being More
• Tired		• Inspired
• Confused		• Clear

BE-DO-HAVE

EXERCISE

Who do I choose to be?

What will I choose to do?

What result do I choose to have?

BE-DO-HAVE

EXERCISE

Who do I choose to be?

I choose to be a successful entrepreneur with a specialty in financial services.

What will I choose to do?

I choose to help people make smart decisions about their money.

What result do I choose to have?

I choose to have financial independence, freedom of choice, and work-life balance.

3

THE POWER OF YOUR
AUTHENTIC INTENTIONS

"I want to know how God created this world. . . .
I want to know His thoughts; the rest are details."
ALBERT EINSTEIN

"Actions produce results in keeping with your intentions."
DR. MARIA NEMETH

BUILDING TO AN AUTHENTIC MINDSET

Be **clear** every intention carries within itself the mechanics for its own fulfillment.

Be **confident** that what you take out of a relationship is in proportion to what you put into it.

Be **capable** of attracting people to you rather than chasing them.

n 1960, a study of business school students began that spanned the next 20 years. Fifteen hundred graduates were asked what they wanted to pursue first after graduation—money or mission? Category A consisted of those graduates who said they wanted to make money first, so that they could do what they really wanted to later. Category B comprised those who would pursue their passion first, secure in the belief that money would eventually follow.

Eighty-three percent of the graduates—1,245 people—fell into Category A, the "money now" group. Category B ("mission now") made up only 17 percent, or 255 of the 1,500 respondents.

By 1980, there were 101 millionaires among the overall group of 1,500. One of them came from Category A. The other 100 were all from Category B, the ones who pursued their passion. The study's author, Srully Blotnick (*Getting Rich Your Own Way*, Doubleday, 1980), concluded that "the overwhelming majority of people who have become wealthy have become so thanks to work they found profoundly absorbing. . . . Their 'luck' arose from the accidental dedication they had to an area they enjoyed."

The intent of this group was to follow their passion and make a difference. Willingness and conviction to their careers characterized their mindset. Given the choice of making money or making a difference, they chose to make a difference. In the end, they accomplished both.

THE POWER OF INTENTIONS

The findings of the business school study dramatically illustrate the power of our intentions. Almost 40 percent of the "mission now" group became extraordinarily wealthy—even though wealth itself was not what they sought. Less than one-tenth of 1 percent of the "money now" group achieved the wealth they were seeking—the external goal they put before all else.

The Law of Intention: Every intention carries within itself the mechanics for its own fulfillment.

Every intention carries within itself the mechanics for its own fulfillment. Let me explain this in practical terms. Think about a situation where you were asked to do something you truly did not want to do. Let's say your spouse asked you to go visit their family on a day that you had other plans for yourself. If you did this against your will, think about what you were thinking, what you were saying, and how you acted once you got there. Your intention was to be somewhere else, so you clearly demonstrated the fact that you did not want to be where you were. Chances are you were whining and complaining all the way there.

You readily see this on a daily basis in the workplace. How many times have you been in the presence of someone who uses kind words, but the intent is to snub someone and that is what cuts through. You also may recognize this when someone gives an expensive gift to another with no love or meaning behind it. The point is, you cannot stop your intention. It will always produce the result of the original thought behind it. Be aware and focus on your intentions; they will drive your behavior.

> **The Law of Reciprocity:** What you take out of a relationship is in proportion to what you put into it.

Think of the intent of someone who is trying to sell you. Where is his or her focus? Is it on you or is it on them? When your intention is to sell someone, you behave one way, and your client will sense it. If your intention is to serve, you act in an altogether different manner, and that will also be evident to your client.

People love to buy and dislike being sold. Pay attention to this simple yet profound truth. When you present yourself in such a way that you are selling, your prospect and client immediately sense that and it creates a negative feeling for them. When you present yourself in a manner that helps them solve their problems or concerns, they sense that as well. Keep in mind that the essence of client creation is that people will *buy* from you based on how they *feel* about you, not what they *think* about you.

ATTENTION ENERGIZES; INTENTION TRANSFORMS

What you put your attention on expands; what you take it away from disappears. Pay attention to the *quality of your intentions*, because what you think about will present itself. For example, if you focus your attention on money, you will observe your saving and spending habits. You will either be pleased at how much you are saving or disappointed by how much potential leakage you have in your personal economy. The same holds true for your relationships. People stay in relationships that focus on the relationships, and leave them when they do not.

In most professions, we are typically taught to pay more attention to our products and their applications than our communication and relationship skills. Yet, a very small percentage of the entire process is based on the product itself. Dale Carnegie, in his now famous book *How to Win Friends and Influence People,* suggested that 85 percent of the sales process is directly related to communication, and the remaining 15 percent is related to product knowledge. Though the facts of this study were revealed in the 1930s, they are as true today as they were then. However, traditional training still places the emphasis on product-based solutions.

You know intuitively that the bulk of the client process is really about the quality of the relationship and communication. When you choose to validate the 85/15 rule and master your own communication and relationship skills, you will dramatically increase your effectiveness in the process of client creation. We have all experienced someone we knew who bought something from someone we viewed as having an inferior product or an inferior company. If you are willing to tell the truth about that situation, you most likely spent more time talking about the product than focusing on the quality of the relationship.

CONTENT VERSUS CONTEXT

Serving others begins with an awareness that everyone has their own level of understanding. Everyone has their own context of your content. For example, ask five people how to define success, and they will each provide a different definition. The content is the word *success;* the context is the various answers you will receive.

The essence of communication is the ability to communicate through someone else's filter of understanding. What something means to you is not necessarily what it means to someone else. When you say something to somebody, it must pass through their filter of what it means to them. When you simply supply facts, you leave it up to the client's perception of what those facts mean. However, when you provide information through their filter, they don't have to guess what you are saying or try to read your mind.

Feelings are especially judged through a person's filter. The projection of how you feel is subject to the other person's perception. What I think I am projecting, and what someone else is perceiving about me, may be completely different. For example, you may believe you are presenting with confidence, while your prospect or client thinks you are extremely arrogant. In the same way, someone may be very passionate about an idea, but their enthusiasm may be perceived as overzealous to someone else.

Be aware that a single word can be perceived in many different ways. What does being authentic mean to you? Your definition is different from everyone else's. It is not right or wrong, but conflict may occur in a relationship when what you are projecting does not align with the perception of the other person. You will learn and grow when you honor and respect the differences of another person.

BEING A PROFESSIONAL

Professionalism is gained by performance, not by your title. A professional exemplifies a positive mental attitude and has a willingness to learn. A professional has the ability to be flexible, adaptable, and improvise when necessary. To me, the most compelling definition of a professional is *someone who performs at their best when they feel like it the least. A professional leaves you feeling served.*

One of the most recognizable attributes of professionals is their willingness to continue to learn. They come from the mindset that they are always in school and can always improve. They are willing to take the time to work on their business, not simply *in* their business. But by far the most important attribute I have ever recognized in top professionals is their teachability or coachability. They are always open and willing to receive feedback and direction.

Think of top-performing athletes like Tiger Woods. Observe the fact that in addition to his incredible work ethic, he always has his coach, Butch Harmon, at his side. He is always willing to accept feedback from his coach and willing to make adjustments. He strives for excellence and not perfection. He focuses attention on the quality of his own game versus the efforts of others. In his mindset, the only competition he has is with himself. He exemplifies a mental toughness as well as physical prowess that is unparalleled. Athletes of the future will not only have to compete with him physically but also mentally. He clearly demonstrates what I call the authentic mindset.

Ask yourself the following: Are you willing versus wanting to do what it takes? Being willing will propel you through those unpleasant tasks that will enhance your performance. I have never been able to help someone effectively, if they were unwilling to be helped or coached. I have observed many people with great talent stay mediocre because of a closed mind or an attitude that they knew everything there was to know about something. In the final analysis, they hit a certain level of performance and stayed at that plateau.

CLIENTS VERSUS CUSTOMERS

What is a client, as opposed to a customer? I define a customer as someone who buys a product or service from you one time and may or may not ever buy from you or see you again. On the other hand, *a client is someone who thinks of you first, last, and always for your product or service.* A client is someone with whom you have created a significant relationship through your authentic intentions and actions. You have been effective in "selling" them once, and then they buy from you over and over again. They do so because you are competent, they like you, and they feel you have their best interests at heart.

> **Client:** Someone who thinks of you first, last, and always for your product or service.

An example of this is the relationship I have with my own attorney, Ira Neiman. I have worked with him for 17 years and consider him first, last, and always for any legal matter I may have. In many cases, my legal requirements may not be within Ira's area of expertise; however, I trust him enough to be in charge of the process, to delegate it to the appropriate associate. The point is, I totally trust his judgment and competence with all of my legal affairs, even when he does not directly get involved. I always feel confident and secure in knowing that he puts my best interests before his own.

This confidence I have in him was further demonstrated when my mother needed her will and trust completed. She interviewed several attorneys in her home state of Florida but would never complete the project. I kept asking her what the problem was, and she said, "I just don't have a good feeling about them." When I visited her in Florida, I went with her on two additional interviews.

Both attorneys did a good job of presenting their services, but my mother remained unimpressed. Finally, on her visit to Chicago, I introduced her to Ira. Within ten minutes in his presence, she tapped me on the arm and whispered in my ear, "I have a very good feeling about him." She immediately instructed him to proceed with any and all necessary documents to complete her planning. Once again, I was reminded of the fact that people buy from people because they *feel* something, not because they *think* something.

WHY PEOPLE CHANGE

From my perspective, *people change for three basic reasons: convenience, crisis, or conviction.*

A classic example of this is health habits. If a person is operating on convenience, they may follow the crowd with whatever fad diet presents itself. Without paying attention to any other factor, they will go along with what everyone else is eating (or not eating). As soon as the fad diet fades, so will their own health goals.

The second reason people change is based on crisis. In the same health example, a crisis scenario, such as a heart attack, would cause someone to change their diet. Given distance from the crisis, the immediate need to keep up with the special diet also dissipates and loses its impact. How many times have you observed someone going back to old behavior patterns after they feel they have "recovered"?

The final reason for change is the only one that will sustain. It is based on conviction. If you seek good health because you would like to have more energy, run a marathon, or simply enjoy your grandchildren and live to see them get married, you will stay the course. You tend to view the result as an *opportunity* to do something positive for yourself or someone else, rather than an obligation to do so. Remember this: *You can never get anyone to do something they really do not want to do.*

Think of the times in your life when these three opportunities for change presented themselves. Ask yourself which one of them sustained your focus and yielded the desired result. Will and discipline alone do not work. This is readily apparent with people who join health clubs in December and, by the end of January, quickly forget why they joined. Change will not sustain until you have the *conviction* to make it so. In your business model, a passion for what you are doing will give you the conviction to change from selling to serving.

The change that stems from conviction is motivated by love—of self and of others. This motivation leads to long-lasting, real change. It comes out of truth and purpose. It is not merely enforced through willpower and discipline but comes out of what you truly desire. It is anchored in an authentic mindset.

The following exercise, called Creating the EDGE (Engage, Develop, Grow, and Empower), is designed to help you think through your intentions with respect to your career. These four questions have helped me and many others think through the important issues regarding their careers.

Ann, one of my coaching clients, has been an agency manager and producer for over ten years, quietly building a strong practice. Looking to increase production, Ann sat down and answered the questions in the EDGE tool after she heard how it had dramatically improved other coaching clients' production. Each question and subsequent answer brought her more clarity and excitement. In ten years of "doing" insurance, she had never taken the time to really understand what talents she would like to develop, how she could measure and sustain her growth, and what she liked best and enjoyed most about her career. With her new clarity, she was able to focus her time on what empowered her and helped her become more aware of the process she was using with clients—not just how many clients she could see. She also used the EDGE tool with her staff to empower her whole team to work more effectively and efficiently. The following quarter, Ann's agency was in the top ten for production in her district for the first time ever.

These questions may not be easy to answer, but they are important to help you reach a clarity about your career, to understand your own view of the vision of your business and not simply take someone else's word for it. Answering these questions can lead you to the heart of why you chose your career and will increase your confidence.

There is space for you to work on your answers followed by my own personal responses as an example. I include in my responses the evolution of my answers over time, where appropriate.

A *u t h e n t i c* **T** *r u t h s*

- Actions produce results in keeping with your intentions.

- People buy from people based on how they *feel* about them and not by what they *think* about them.

- People change for three reasons: convenience, crisis, or conviction.

EXERCISE	
ENGAGE **E**	Why did you choose your career?
DEVELOP **D**	What talents would you like to develop?
GROW **G**	How do you measure and sustain your growth?
EMPOWER **E**	What do you like best and enjoy most about your career?

EXERCISE	
ENGAGE	Why did you choose your career?
E	*Initially, I chose professional sales and marketing because it provided me with the prospect of unlimited income potential and unlimited opportunity.* *Now I see my career as an opportunity to help others bring their life to their business to bring their business to life.*
DEVELOP	What talents would you like to develop?
D	*Initially, I wanted to enhance my communication and relationship skills to better serve my clients, family, and coworkers.* *Now, I would like to expand on my opportunity to coach and mentor others. I choose to motivate and inspire people through my speaking, teaching, and writing.*
GROW	How do you measure and sustain your growth?
G	*Early in my career, I measured my growth by what I had—more specifically, the visible signs of material wealth.* *Now, I focus on what I will become as a result of my life experiences and the legacy I will leave behind.*
EMPOWER	What do you like best and enjoy most about your career?
E	*Initially, I was passionate about helping people become better educated, more organized, and better prepared for the financial issues they had to face.* *Now, I enjoy speaking, teaching, creating innovative materials, and sharing what I have learned with others to help them do what they do best and do it to the best of their ability.*

4

DISCOVERING YOUR VALUE

*"Your work is to discover your work, and
then with all your heart give yourself to it."*
BUDDHA

"We discover ourselves through others."
CARL JUNG

BUILDING TO AN AUTHENTIC MINDSET

Be **clear** your values and qualities make the difference.

Be **confident** about what you can deliver.

Be **capable** of aligning your intentions with actions.

Ask yourself the question, Why am I attracted to some people and not to others? Each of us has a certain style and presents a certain personality. We all have those special relationships with which we "click" and have great chemistry. On the other hand, we have all been in the presence of people who turn us off like a light switch.

In order for you to present yourself effectively to others, you must first be clear on the values and qualities that you demonstrate in their presence. This is critical to understand, as these values and qualities will guide your actions and behavior. So many times, we engage people and walk away either feeling we like them or don't like them, without fully understanding why or how we came to this conclusion.

THE VCR FILTER

Whenever we engage someone, there is an unconscious filter we place this person and their personality through. In essence, we all ask the same question: "Who are you, and how will I benefit from knowing you?" On contact, our minds boot up like a super-fast computer and scan the visual and vocal information we receive. It has been said that women put someone through their intuitive filter in about 17 seconds, and men in about 37 seconds. The next thing we say will either confirm or deny their initial perception of us.

Think about what you consider when you engage someone professionally and personally. I think this information will serve you best if you consistently look at things from your own perspective. Once you lock on to this important understanding, you can then consciously monitor your behavior to effectively engage with others.

The three filters that you would consider in establishing a relationship with anyone are the following:

1. The **V**alue of the opportunity
2. The **C**onfidence in the relationship
3. The **R**esult that may occur

Let's look at an example of how this may work in your life on a regular basis. Suppose for the moment, a good friend of yours called and said that he had met someone who had dramatically increased productivity and effectiveness in his business. He further implied that he thought of you while working with this individual and suggested the two of you meet to discuss his services. Think about how you might respond to his offer.

The first filter you consider is the *value of the opportunity*. You most likely will initially ask yourself how you feel about your current business and productivity and will quickly arrive at a feeling about it. You may think you are doing extremely well and do not need to meet, or you may value the ideas and become curious.

The second filter will be your *confidence in the relationship* with the person that called you. If you value their opinion, professionalism, and character, and, more important, respect who they are, it will influence your decision.

The third filter is the *result that may occur*. You quickly assess the risk-reward equation associated with meeting this person. If you view the opportunity as a distraction, taking you away from your other responsibilities, you most likely will choose not to meet. If, on the other hand, you see the result as potentially positive in that you can gain from the opportunity, you may tell your friend, "Have him give me a call."

As you can appreciate, this whole decision-making process takes place in less than a minute. Your mind scans your entire database of thoughts, feelings, and emotions and makes a decision immediately. If you have a red light on any of these filters, you most likely will simply tell your friend, "Thank you; however, I do not feel the need to meet with him at this time."

Why is it so important to pay attention to this key concept? Because you utilize this VCR filter with virtually every decision you make. Not only do you put people through these three filters, you also do it with every opportunity that comes your way. You are doing it right now as you read this book. You looked at the title, and it piqued your interest or sparked your curiosity. More specifically, you asked yourself, What is in it for me, and how can I benefit from reading this book? You most likely checked my credentials and credibility to see if I know what I'm talking about. Finally, you assessed the risk-reward of taking the time to read the book to obtain new ideas.

The reason this VCR filter is so key is that every person you meet is placing you through these filters. Each person, on meeting with you, is assessing the *value of the opportunity,* their *confidence* in who you are, and the *risk-reward* of meeting with you. This will more commonly be associated with the risk of selling them something versus the reward of serving.

Setting Your VCR

If you are a baby boomer, like myself, chances are you purchased a videocassette recorder machine (VCR) in the 1980s. Remember how complicated it was to simply set the time, by going through no less than 20 steps, utilizing a remote control with 50 buttons? It is almost comical to me to think how many homes I went into where I saw 12:00 flashing on every VCR. No one seemed to want to take the time or make the effort to learn how to set the time on their VCR.

For so many of us, that's how we initially show up at client meetings. We seldom set our personal VCR filters, which results in not being clear on our value to someone else, not being confident in what we can deliver, or not understanding why we get the result we do. Although manufacturers of VCR machines made the improvement to automatically set the time, those of us in professional services must do this manually.

The best way I can serve you and help you to assess your value, reinforce your confidence, and obtain a favorable result with someone, is to coach you through the process rather than simply tell you. The VCR filter tool at the end of this chapter will serve as your template to follow. You may want to make a reference copy to work with as we go along. Let me help you by walking you through each component and explaining its purpose. This tool is vital to your personal understanding and will subsequently be used in Chapter 5 to build on what is working in your current relationships. In Chapter 6, we will build on this information once again to produce your *Personal Value Statement.* Completion of this exercise will culminate in producing a powerful statement of who you are and why people should work with you.

Values: The beliefs and standards that guide our intentions and actions.

The first step of the process is to complete the "Values" section. Allow yourself no more than ten minutes to complete this section. Scan the list of values and qualities that is presented. As you observe this list, please feel free to add any others that may work for you. Your objective here is to select ten values and qualities that you resonate with and define them in your own terms. This is very important, for as I stated earlier, we each have our own context of what something means to us. For example, one of my values is freedom, which I define in my own terms to mean "the power to choose." I encourage you to place the words *I am* in front of the value or quality to see how it resonates with you. You will observe that you either align with the word or do not. Do not judge this; simply notice how you feel about it.

The second step in the values category is to take the top six from your list of ten and then prioritize them accordingly. I encourage you to look at these six values and qualities in another way. If I suggest to you that you only have six words to describe who you are and how you define yourself, which words will you pick? These are the words you're looking for.

If I now suggest to you that you can only define yourself in three words, take the top three from your six and prioritize them. Finally, if you can only define yourself in one word or be known to demonstrate this one value or quality, what will it be? This one value, or your moral compass, is the one that is more important than all others. This lead value is the one that will drive the choices you make in your life.

Let's take a moment and reflect on what you just completed. I want you to observe something very important and very compelling. I would like you to take a look at the six values that you listed and ask yourself the following: How many of the sustaining and significant relationships in my life are that way because of having similar values and qualities?

The compelling point for you to understand is the values and qualities that you exemplify to other people are what make you attractive to them. *People align with others who share the same values* and, therefore, choose to engage with you professionally or personally. You observe this on a regular basis when these "significant" client relationships also become good friendships. This is not by accident. This is because you trust each other and tell each other the truth.

Friend: A person who will always tell you the truth.

Confidence: The ability to think clearly, communicate effectively, and take authentic action.

The next part of the tool is to complete the "Confidence" section. I am of strong belief that nothing is more important than to reinforce your confidence on a regular basis. I define confidence as the ability to think clearly, communicate effectively, and take authentic action.

In this section, I would like to have you focus on your best client relationships and think through what you confidently deliver to them. In other words, what actions do you take that are consistent with the values you have mentioned above? Think of those situations where there is no doubt in your mind about how you will act. You are confident that you will or will not do these things.

For example, if one of your values is empathy, the action you may take is to seek to understand before being understood. Another action may be that you are a good listener. If trust is a lead value for you, the actions may be to tell the truth and be reliable and dependable with people.

The important thing here is to pay attention to how the value will produce the desired behavior. List as many as you can and then pick the top three actions that you feel your clients align with. Put yourself in their place for the moment and think about how they may answer the question, What actions do I confidently demonstrate to you?

Keep this information readily available and in your mind, for it will become the basis for a deeper understanding in Chapter 5 as to why people work with you. For now, I simply want you to identify and be confident about what you deliver to people on a regular basis.

> **Result:** The outcome produced when actions are aligned with intentions.

Now complete the "Results" section by thinking through your answer to this question: What are the feelings exchanged in my best relationships? If you were to ask your sustaining and significant relationships how you make them feel through your values and actions, what would they say? Remember, the essence of client creation is people connecting with people based on how they feel about them not what they think about them. Through your projection of your values, qualities, and actions, what is being perceived about you?

For example, in the Financial Services industry feelings determine purchases. People are writing a check for something intrinsically worth very little, such as the paper it is written on. What feelings do you want your prospects and clients to walk away with? Pay attention, because in essence this is your *real* product. Your best clients would most likely tell you that you make them feel confident, secure, comfortable, have peace of mind, etc. List as many feelings as you can and, once again, identify the top three feelings you want your clients to perceive about you.

On the flip side, there also may be a perceived risk in working with you that is commonly called the FUD factor (Fear, Uncertainty, and Doubt). Identify what these feelings may be. For example, if you are a relatively new financial rep in your career, a perceived risk may be that you simply do not have the experience to serve a mature client. Another example of this may be if you project too much confidence to someone, they may perceive it as arrogance. If you project too much passion about something, the perception may be that you are overzealous.

In so many cases, what we think we are projecting and what is perceived by the prospect or client are totally different. I have observed in these situations that the very reason some people engage with us (our strengths) are the very reason that they will disconnect when we turn these qualities up a notch.

Discovering and aligning your values and qualities will make all the difference in your ability to attract quality prospects and clients. What this could mean to you is to have more impact in your relationships. The real benefit is that you will be capable of aligning your authentic intentions and values with your actions.

A u t h e n t i c   T r u t h s

The VCR filter is the filter through which you would consider engaging with anyone:

- The *value* of the opportunity.
- The *confidence* in the relationship.
- The *result* that may occur.

SETTING YOUR VCR

TOOL

Value: The beliefs and standards that guide our intentions and actions.*

Abundance	Consciousness	Gentleness	Justice	Questions
Authenticity	Contribution	Grace	Kaizen	Respect
Beauty	Courage	Harmony	Kindness	Rewards
Bliss	Creativity	Honesty	Leadership	Sacredness
Calling	Destiny	Honor	Learning	Self-esteem
Cause	Detachment	Hope	Legacy	Service
Chemistry	Effectiveness	Humility	Love	Simplicity
Communication	Empathy	Infusion	Motivation	Spontaneity
Community	Encouragement	Inspiration	Openness	Success
Congruence	Equality	Integration	Partnership	Teamwork
	Faith	Integrity	Profit	Trust
VALUE	Flow	Intimacy	Promise keeping	Truthfulness
	Forgiveness	Intuition	Prosperity	Vision
	Freedom	Joy	Purpose	Wisdom

*Add any others that work for you

Confidence: The ability to think clearly, communicate effectively, and take authentic action.

CONFIDENCE

C

EXAMPLES: I am reliable and dependable.
I am a good listener.
I am a good communicator.

Result: Actions produce results in keeping with your intentions.

RESULT

R

Reward	Risk
Enhanced	Limited
Utilized	Exploited
Appreciated	Manipulated

SETTING YOUR VCR

TOOL

Choose ten values/qualities and explain something about what they mean to you.

VALUE/QUALITY   MEANING   PRIORITIZE YOUR LIST OF VALUES

_____   _____   1 _____   1 _____   1 _____

_____   _____   2 _____   2 _____

_____   _____   3 _____   3 _____

_____   _____   4 _____

_____   _____   5 _____

_____   _____   6 _____

_____   _____

_____   _____   ➡️   **PRIMARY VALUE**

_____   _____

_____   _____   The one value that is more important than all others.
It is the one that drives the choices you make.

What are you confident about that you can deliver? _____

_____

_____

_____

What feelings are exchanged in these relationships?

Reward   Risk

_____   _____

_____   _____

_____   _____

_____   _____

_____   _____

5

KNOWING WHY PEOPLE
WORK WITH YOU

"Knowing others is wisdom. Knowing yourself is enlightenment."
LAO TZU

*"Experience is not what happens to you.
It's what you do with what happens to you."*
ALDOUS HUXLEY

BUILDING TO AN AUTHENTIC MINDSET

Be **clear** people buy from people, not from companies.

Be **confident** people will exchange a check for a feeling.

Be **capable** of knowing what works and what does not work in your relationships.

Think about your significant relationships and what makes them authentic, reciprocal, and sustaining. Why do these people work with you, and what keeps them engaged? Perhaps it is appropriate here to remind you of what I stated earlier, that *all relationships are a reflection of the one you have with yourself.*

I was meeting with a client I had been working with for more than 20 years. As our meeting wrapped up, he turned to me check in hand and asked, "Who should I make this out to?" Through years of meetings, planning, and portfolios, this person had looked to me. I had not changed companies since we started working together, and the company name was clearly on the portfolio I had just presented to him. In his eyes, I was what he was buying. This clearly confirms what many of us know, that *people buy from people, not from companies.*

This simple truth is evident in every industry. When you think about it, corporations are nothing more than a collection of individuals who make or break your first impression. Although they may represent a company, their presence supersedes that of the organization. You have experienced this many times. Think of your airline of choice, your favorite hotel or restaurant, your bank teller, limo driver, store clerk, and the list goes on and on. These businesses and services are nothing more than buildings and establishments made up of people—people you connect with and who convey a positive feeling to you.

In order to better understand the power of attractor patterns, I did the most courageous thing I have ever done in my career. In 1987, after six years of private practice, I wrote a letter to my top 200 clients for feedback as to why they chose to work with me. I sent a letter, a survey, and a stamped return envelope and held my breath. The letter suggested that in order for me to provide quality service to them, I encouraged their candid feedback and comments on my professionalism. The questions I posed to them were the following:

- Why did you choose to engage with me?
- What values/qualities do we share?
- How have I exemplified these values/qualities?
- In three words, how do you feel about our relationship?
- Do you have suggestions for improvement?

I received back 187 surveys within 30 days. The information was powerful and life changing. This information is typically not shared between the client and advisor and usually remains unknown. More commonly, we usually have no relationship-based communication with our clients until a meltdown occurs and there seems to be a problem. Keep this very important thought in mind: *If you want something you have never had, you will have to do something you have never done.* I will repeatedly bring up this key concept throughout this book to remind you of the tremendous opportunities in front of you at this time in your career.

The findings of my initial survey revealed what I intuitively knew. The reasons they chose to engage with me were mainly relationship-based responses, such as:

- I was empathetic to their situation.
- I educated them.
- I showed respect to them and their assets.
- I helped them solve problems.
- I had lots of great ideas.
- I kept in touch with them on a regular basis.

The values and qualities that we shared were clear, confident, capable, caring, considerate, determined, educating, energetic, ethical, generous, helpful, honest, optimistic, polite, respectful, responsible, sharing, thoughtful, trusting, truthful, and warm.

Note that these clients responded and were attracted to these powerful patterns of behavior. The key point is that they reflected on the values we *shared,* meaning they themselves owned and demonstrated these values and qualities. In order to recognize a quality in another, you must first recognize it in yourself.

In the demonstration of these values and qualities, they indicated responses such as:

- I educated, organized, and prepared them for the issues they faced.
- I was a resource for their financial security.
- I helped take the "ifs" out of their lives.

- I helped them connect to what they deeply cared about.
- I helped them make intelligent decisions regarding their finances.

These responses conveyed to me how the original intentions converted to actions that the client perceived as valuable. This is an extremely important element, as it ultimately comes down to how you act with people, not what you say to them.

In asking how they felt about our relationship, they shared responses such as comfortable, confident, served, trusting, respectful, open, flexible, and significant. There was absolutely no doubt why these clients wrote checks for my services. The truth is, in virtually every situation, *people exchange a check for a feeling.*

Finally, in the area of improvement or opportunity to enhance professionalism, I gained a new understanding. They shared such things as sometimes I could be arrogant—translation, *too confident.* They shared that I could be impulsive and want to move along too quickly—translation, *too energetic.* They shared that I could be too ambitious—translation, *my desire-to-serve attitude could overwhelm them.* In every case, the values and qualities they perceived that they liked about me were the same ones that could create a disconnect when I projected too much of them.

In Chapter 4, I suggested that you focus on discovering your value to others by establishing your VCR filter. This, once again, is the ability to pay attention to how people assess the value of working with you, the confidence they have in your actions, and the result in the form of a feeling perceived about you. Developing a clear understanding of these vital elements will keep you out of pain and in your authentic mindset.

Pain has many faces. It shows itself in the form of crisis, concern, dissatisfaction, disappointment, fear, or frustration. Pain causes you to come home feeling burnt out and tired. It causes you to turn away from your friends and family when they want to engage you. It is pain that causes you to snap at your loved ones after a "bad day at the office." Who are you really mad at? Intuitively, you are mad at yourself, because you know you acted without integrity. When you start consciously focusing on what is working in your relationships and why people work with you, it will produce what I call your *integrity quotient*. I define integrity quotient as the ability to recognize the difference between the truth you know and the truth you live.

Integrity quotient: The ability to recognize the difference between the truth you know and the truth you live.

Keep in mind you are about to make a very important choice. You can consciously or unconsciously attract people to you. *Your career right now is the sum total of all the choices you have made to date.*

Choice: A decision one makes to either avoid or create a particular outcome.

THE REASONS CLIENTS LEAVE

In 1991, I conducted a survey of 200 entrepreneurs to obtain the flip side of my 1987 survey. I was mainly interested to learn why these potential prospects and clients would *not* engage with a financial professional. I kept my survey independent and neutral, so that the people were compelled to provide truthful feedback and could be safe with their responses. Their answers were filtered down and distilled into three main reasons why they would not engage. I will use the VCR filter format here to help you readily connect with the findings:

- *Value:* Lack of unique difference. Respondents felt the professionals could not communicate a unique value or difference with what they already had done.
- *Confidence:* Lack of understanding. Respondents had very little confidence in the ability of the professional to commu-

nicate in their terms. They found the advisor confusing and too technical in their delivery.

- *Result:* Lack of likeability and trust. Respondents felt they were being "sold" and that *their best interests* were not being served.

My study revealed compelling information that I utilized in my private practice and in my workshops. This information should remind all of us that our prospects are looking for the differences, not likenesses, in our delivery system. These prospects or clients are continually making choices and decisions about our value. I would have you consider this: *In order for a prospect to hire you, in almost every case someone else has to be fired.* When in doubt, if they see no added value, a tie will stay with the incumbent advisor. You know that your existing clients are being contacted by other financial services professionals on a regular basis. How are you currently protecting and securing your relationships? Think about it.

THE ESSENCE OF CREDIBILITY

You can lose all of your money, and someone can lend you more money. However, if you lose your credibility, no friends or colleagues can lend you theirs. You cannot *borrow* someone else's credibility to have your phone calls returned and have people desire to meet with you.

This lack of credibility and sense of betrayal in the workplace is everywhere these days. We witness the business debacles of the past few years, and how certain individuals violate trust and confidence and bring huge corporations crashing down around them. According to a study in the July 22, 2002, issue of *Forbes* ("Bad Boys in Business" by Daniel Lyons), an astounding 46 percent of Americans admit that they are acting at work in a way they would never even think of acting at home. The values they demonstrate at work are completely different from those they want their loved ones to witness. Many people are indeed acting without integrity and not aligning their so-called intentions and values with their actions and behavior.

Dan Sullivan, the founder and president of The Strategic Coach program, has advocated habits essential in being referable. These habits are:

- Show up on time.
- Do what you say.
- Finish what you start.
- Say "please" and "thank you" to people.

I would suggest that these habits are even more compelling if you look at them from the vantage point of credibility. People are referable because of their credibility. You have all experienced this personally and professionally. There are certain industries and professions notorious for not showing up on time, not doing what they say, or not finishing what they start in a timely manner. No matter how good we may be at our profession or craft, we can always see the hesitancy in making an introduction or referring people like that to someone else.

Ask yourself the tough question, Am I referable? How would your clients introduce you, and what would they do if they saw you walking down the street while they were with their best friend? Would they stop and introduce you or avoid you? Do you have credibility with your staff and associates? Look inside yourself and be truthful at this time in your career.

An example of establishing credibility with my staff was a situation where a client was speaking in a demeaning manner to my director of marketing without my knowledge. She did not tell me about it, because I had just earned a $60,000 commission from this client, which she did not want to jeopardize. However, at one point after a discussion with this client, she approached me and said she could no longer work with him and asked me to call him directly. As I attempted to find out the reason, she simply said, "I would prefer not to work with him." I finally was able to draw out of her that he had been speaking to her in a demeaning way, making her extremely uncomfortable.

Without hesitation, I drove to the client's office, walked in unannounced, and asked him to apologize to my assistant for his behavior. He denied that he was offensive and refused to apologize. I told him that he left me no choice but to resign as his advisor and assign another representative, with the knowledge that I would have to return the commission I had earned and already received. When I returned to the office, I informed my staff that I had resigned from the client, because they were more important to me than he was. I may have lost a client, but I did the right thing for the people who matter most to me. An interesting note about this case, the client never cancelled his program.

Your credibility will be challenged all the time. Getting clear on this concept of credibility is the first step towards better relationships. You choose to make the commitment to understand why people work with you and observe what works and what doesn't work in your current relationships. *In order for you to start doing something positive, you must stop doing something negative.* It is important that you examine your internal beliefs about your relationships and examine those behaviors that are no longer effective and working. You cannot modify your behavior without first addressing your underlying belief about it.

Think about your significant relationships and what makes them authentic, reciprocal, and sustaining. As you define what values and qualities attracted you to these people, go back to your VCR filter and look at your list of values. Identify your top six values and see how they align with the values you are listing in this current exercise.

It is important to fill in the whys yourself, but feedback from others also is crucial to really understanding why people work with you. Connect back to the VCR filter. One of the best ways I know to effectively learn *why* my relationships are significant, *what* values and qualities I share with others, and *how* we make each other feel is to ask my top relationships. I have provided you with a sample survey that was sent to 200 of my clients in order to understand how I could enhance my process and value to them. If you are willing to do the same, you will be rewarded with a great learning experience. Remember, if you want to improve the results with your clients, be willing to improve yourself.

This is your chance to learn how others see you, and what makes you valuable to them. The feedback they provide will create clarity and confidence for both of you.

A u t h e n t i c **T** r u t h s

- In order for you to be hired, in almost every case, someone else has to be fired.

- Your career right now is the sum total of all the choices you have made to date.

- If you want something you have never had, you will have to do something you have never done.

KNOW WHAT HAS WORKED IN YOUR RELATIONSHIPS

SURVEY

Name _____

Date _____ Years Known _____ ❑ Personal ❑ Professional

Why did you choose to engage with me?_____

_____
_____
_____
_____

What values/qualities do we share? _____

_____
_____
_____
_____

How have I exemplified these values/qualities? _____

_____
_____
_____
_____

In three words, how do you feel about our relationship? _____

_____
_____
_____
_____

KNOW WHAT HAS WORKED

EXERCISE

Think about your significant relationships and what makes them authentic, reciprocal, and sustaining.

Who do you respect and admire? _____

_____

What values and qualities attracted you to them? _____

_____

How does this person make you feel? _____

_____

_____

_____

Who do you respect and admire? _____

_____

What values and qualities attracted you to them? _____

_____

_____

How does this person make you feel? _____

_____

_____

_____

Who do you respect and admire? _____

_____

What values and qualities attracted you to them? _____

_____

_____

How does this person make you feel? _____

_____

_____

6

COMMUNICATING CLEARLY, EFFECTIVELY, AND WITH PURPOSE

*"You have the creative power of the universe
on the tip of your tongue."*
A COURSE IN MIRACLES

"Words are, of course, the most powerful drug used by mankind."
RUDYARD KIPLING

BUILDING TO AN AUTHENTIC MINDSET

Be **clear** you are paid to communicate.

Be **confident** in the power of your words.

Be **capable** of communicating who you are, what you will do, and how that serves others.

You have the creative power of the universe on the tip of your tongue.

Read this incredibly powerful statement again and think of the implications. Think about a time when someone has said something to you that either lifted you to great heights or plunged you to the depths. We have all been on the giving and receiving end of compliments and insults and know how just one powerful word can change our mood and how we view ourselves dramatically. Words have power. After your thoughts, your words are the second level of your ability to create experiences.

YOU ARE PAID TO COMMUNICATE

In a professional role, you are paid to communicate. Your ability to earn money is in direct proportion to your ability to communicate your value. The most important question you are asked on a regular basis—"Who are you?"—is far too often misunderstood and discounted. It happens on a regular basis. The question sneaks up on you no matter where you are—at a business meeting, a family event, a cocktail party, or a Little League game—*"What do you do?"* These are four little words with powerful implications. Think of the times you have asked others this question. What are you really asking them? What you are really asking is, "Who are you, and why should I consider talking to you?"

What do you do? A question only you can answer and, in my experience, the most important question you will ever answer. It presents an opportunity to express yourself or depress yourself. It is an opportunity to attract someone to you or repel them from you. It allows you to be interesting or very boring. It is a chance to shine or a chance to whine. How do you feel right now about the way you answer this question?

The way that you respond to this question reflects your belief about your work and your life. Somewhere, somehow, somebody determined that we should answer this question with a label and nothing more—I am a banker, I am a lawyer, I am a salesperson. Not only do we tend to label ourselves and leave others to judge what that means, but we also discount our own labels. How many times have you heard someone answer with "I'm *just* a salesman"? Perhaps you have even said something like this yourself. Ultimately, you are sending the message that you do not see the value in who you are and what you do. I experienced this in countless situations in my workshops. Developing and experienced professionals alike will break eye contact and go to a place of pain with their responses. They are extremely uncomfortable with how they respond to the question. I remind them that if they don't think they are good enough, why would they expect anyone else to think differently. This terrible habit of labeling ourselves so often leaves us feeling diminished and unfulfilled. I have found only one effective benefit to a label in my career. If I do not wish to engage with someone, all I have to do is say "I'm a life insurance salesman" and the discussion is over.

Remember, the essence of attracting anyone is paying attention to what is going on inside of you. If your answer to the question is muddled, ambivalent, or uninspired, then your prospects and clients will pick up on that. If you respond in a compelling manner and state a cause for your work, it can become a powerful magnet that draws others to you. Think about how you are drawn to a good cause. You can respond with a statement of who you are, what you will do, and how that will serve others in a manner that creates a powerful cause that your clients will align with. You do not have to pitch yourself or hustle yourself; you only have to communicate the magic of your vision expressed through your words.

THE POWER OF THE PERSONAL VALUE STATEMENT

This is the most important concept and tool in this entire book. If you take nothing away but this idea and act on it, it will dramatically impact your ability to attract prospects and convert them into clients. The benefits of creating your Personal Value Statement (PVS) are the following:

- **Your PVS states who you are, what you will do, and how you will serve others clearly, effectively, and with pur-**

pose. You will be able to attract people who are aligned with your values and qualities in 30 seconds or less.

- **Your PVS sets your intentions, actions, and results for the relationship.** Every intention carries within itself the mechanics for its own fulfillment. When you state the reasons why people should work with you, you will act that way.
- **Your PVS attracts others to your cause or purpose and will motivate and inspire you.** Stating a cause is more powerful than labeling yourself.
- **Your PVS provides the opportunity for your clients, staff, and family to market you effectively.** You can build a distribution channel of people who can effectively communicate your value.

"IF YOU BUILD IT, THEY WILL COME"

Remember what I said earlier: You are paid to communicate and to be confident in the power of your words. Although you ultimately may deliver your Personal Value Statement in 30 seconds, it will require the initial effort of doing the internal work necessary to create a compelling statement. It is also important to note that this statement must be authentic and represent your values and qualities. If you simply choose to memorize someone else's statement and do not own it, it will impact the delivery and appear disingenuous. The key is to use your own words and describe your own actions. By doing so, you will internalize this statement, play to your strengths, and get significant results very quickly.

Mike R., a broker, put together his PVS and shared with me that he was using it inconsistently and getting inconsistent results. I asked him to share his statement with me and go over each element individually, so that we could see what was potentially blocking him. We went over his initial values, and I asked him why he chose these. He said, "because those were values I thought people wanted to hear." When I asked him if those were his lead values, he said they were not. This gave us our first clue as to why he was inconsistent in delivering his statement. He did not have the confidence to deliver it, because it was something that he was memorizing and had not internalized as his own. We went back and had him write down what his three lead values were, how he demonstrated those values, and, ultimately, how he wanted people to feel after they worked with him. I could instantly see the excitement on his face as he wrote down exactly who he was. He then went out and shared this authentic value statement, delivering it confidently and consistently. In the 30 days after our session, he produced one of the most effective and productive months in his career.

If you have completed the exercises in Chapters 4 and 5, you are virtually prepared to create the first draft of your initial Personal Value Statement. In the VCR filter exercise, I asked you to articulate your lead values. Follow along with a separate sheet of paper or refer to the tool, "Why People Work with You," at the end of this chapter. Your first action is to list the three values you feel represent who you are and place them in the first section, entitled "People work with me because . . . " You also may want to write down the meaning of the value as well.

The second step is to record the three top actions you are confident you can deliver in the "What This Means" category of the Personal Value Statement tool. These actions should be configured to the values and serve as a demonstration of what this value means. For example, if a value you select is empathy, this action may be converted to "be a good listener" or "understand before being understood." Do not worry about perfecting these actions or building your cause right now, for it will develop as you drill down and practice.

The third step is to place the feelings exchanged in the relationship from the "Result" category of the VCR filter tool and "The Benefit Is" category of the Personal Value Statement tool. You obviously want to showcase the positive feelings conveyed in your relationships. You may cross-reference to the "Know What

Has Worked" tool in Chapter 5, which articulated the feelings that you received from your most significant relationships. Check to align these feelings and see if they are consistent with what you wish to project to prospects and clients.

Our relationships are our greatest tool to help remind us of who we really are. A great way to gather the information to create your Personal Value Statement is to ask your top ten clients and friends why they work with you and why they associate with you. You can literally feed the questions to them with the example provided in Chapter 5. This is a great way to get truthful feedback from people who know you best and who mean the most to you.

I remember one of my clients commenting that he felt he had thought through the questions and his answers enough that he could "eulogize" me. We both had a good laugh; however, it really made me think about how significant his statement was. We so infrequently communicate our real feelings to each other and oftentimes wait until it is too late. At a funeral service, people never talk about a person's net worth; they talk about how worthy the person was through living their values and qualities.

THE PERSONAL VALUE STATEMENT IN ACTION

The Story of Chuck L., Financial Representative

Chuck was on a plane trip with his wife, flying out to visit some friends. As conversations normally go on a plane, the gentleman sitting next to Chuck started off with some pleasantries on how nice a day it was and where he was going. Then he asked the magic question, "So tell me, what do you do?" Now, Chuck had just gone through my workshop a couple of weeks before and was eager to share his PVS but was still working through changing his normal answer, "I'm a financial services representative." So with a nervous grin, he leaned in and shared his value statement. This opened up a dialogue between Chuck and the prospect that led him to talk about planning needs and goals he had never shared with anyone.

At the end of the flight, Chuck and his new friend exchanged handshakes and business cards, and Chuck promised to get in touch when he returned to the office. In addition, the two men sitting behind Chuck on the plane asked for his card, as they had overheard the entire conversation and really connected with how Chuck had shared his value and the type of questions he had asked. Now, this was a new experience for Chuck, as he usually did not attract so many people to what he did, especially not on a plane trip. The amazing part came on the return trip. Chuck and his wife sat in their seats for the normal preflight routine, when a flight attendant came up and asked the person sitting next to Chuck if he would mind switching his seat. Apparently, she had been the flight attendant on Chuck's first flight and had heard his value statement and really connected with him. She owned properties she was interested in selling and was looking for planning assistance from someone she could trust. She had looked into when Chuck would be making his return flight, booked a standby seat on the same flight, and for the remaining two-hour flight shared the details of her investments and dreams for the future.

The moral of the story is, on what normally would have been a pretty uneventful flight, Chuck had attracted four new prospects and taken two fact finders—all because he had shared his PVS with one person.

Let's look at some sample Personal Value Statements and their applications. The important thing to observe in these statements are the bridges, which create the transitions from your intentions to your actions to your results. The bridges are:

- People work with me because . . . (intentions through values)
- What this means . . . (actions you confidently deliver)
- The benefit is . . . (the result: feelings shared in a relationship)

Personal Value Statement of Brian S.

People choose to work with me, *because* I genuinely understand and appreciate who they are and serve as a resource to help them commit to living a life that works. *What this means* is that I create a safe environment to help you break down your principles and patterns of success and provide the strength of relationship to help you break through to consistently realize your true potential. *The benefit* is the genuine excitement and overwhelming joy of moving forward on a plan that serves you and the people you care most about.

Personal Value Statement of Annette B.

For over five years, people have chosen to work with me, *because* of my passion, patience, and sense of purpose I bring to my clients. *What this means* is that I am excited to build a plan around your vision and goals and help you to experience the life you dream about. *The benefit* is the confidence and excitement to take action and move in the direction of what serves you.

Personal Value Statement of Cliff C.

For over 20 years, business owners and entrepreneurs have chosen to work with me, *because* I care about creating significant client relationships. *What this means* is that I focus on what matters most to you and your family and build a plan around solving your greatest challenges and taking advantage of your greatest opportunities. *The benefit* is that you will have the peace of mind to know you have a financial partner with your best interests in mind.

Personal Value Statement of Ann W.

For over 14 years, my clients have chosen to work with me, *because* I am dedicated to being a resource of clarity and confidence in their personal and professional life. *What this means* is that I will create an environment where you feel comfortable talking about your greatest challenges and opportunities. I will ask you questions that will help both of us get clear on how we can create a balanced plan for you and your family. *The benefit* is that you will have peace of mind to know we are creating a life plan around what matters most to you.

Personal Value Statement of Sebastian M.

For over 15 years, my clients have chosen to work with me, *because* I respect them and am committed to do what is best for them in all circumstances. *What this means* is that I help my clients to connect with what they deeply care about, and I introduce them to a process that motivates them to take action. *The benefit* is that my clients have peace of mind and the security that comes with accomplishing their personal financial goals and objectives.

One of the benefits of the Personal Value Statement is that it provides the capability to attract others to your cause or purpose and inspires you to action. Let me share with you an example of how practical and adaptable the PVS is. My daughter, Danielle, who was running for class president, asked for my assistance in writing a speech to be presented to her class. She observed that I had helped her older sister and brother prepare their winning campaign speeches. I shared with her that the secret is to develop a statement that will promote her in a quick and effective manner. Here is her winning speech:

> Hello, my name is Danielle Cassara, and I am choosing to run for president of Freshman Board because I ap-

preciate and respect who you are as a freshman class. What that means to you is that I will show a genuine interest in the concerns of our class, the opportunities that we might have together, and focus on our unique abilities that can be contributed to our school. The real benefit is that I seek to remind all of us of the important role that we can play in the development of our class culture over the next year. On a personal note, I would like to let you know that it is truly a pleasure to have the opportunity to be a part of a great group of students like you. Thank you.

Finally, let me share with you why over 4,500 people have chosen me as their coach—and why I get up in the morning.

Personal Value Statement of Lou Cassara

People choose to work with me as a coach, *because* I guide them to their greatness through my passion, dedication, and wisdom. *What this means* to those I serve is that I share a process of successful achievement that encourages them to be a first-rate version of themselves. *The benefit* is the clarity and confidence they have to do what they do best and do it to the best of their ability.

A u t h e n t i c   T r u t h s

- You have the creative power of the universe on the tip of your tongue.

- You are paid to communicate.

- Relationships are your greatest tool to help remind you of who you really are.

PERSONAL VALUE STATEMENT

EXERCISE

Develop your initial Personal Value Statement™ using the "Setting Your VCR" worksheet.

People work with me because . . . (your values and qualities)

_____

_____

_____

_____

_____

What this means is . . . (things you deliver confidently)

_____

_____

_____

_____

_____

The benefit is . . . (feelings shared in the relationship)

_____

_____

_____

_____

_____

SAMPLE VALUE STATEMENTS

Personal Value Statement™
Example: "(client's name), for over 21 years, people have chosen to work with me because I care about them and serve as a resource for their clarity and confidence. What this means to the people I serve is that I share a genuine interest in helping them connect with what they deeply care about and provide them with the capability to align their intentions with their actions. The benefit is I'm there to remind them of their importance and the significant difference they make in the lives of others."

Company Value Statement
Example: "One of the ways that I provide the value of expert guidance to you is through my affiliation with (company name). What this means is I have access to world-class companies and specialists who could provide innovative solutions in the areas of personal and business planning. The benefit to you is through these relationships I can serve you and your planning needs by providing a choice of quality companies, products, and services."

Process Value Statement
Example: "My planning process is designed to educate, organize, and prepare my clients for the inevitable financial issues that they will face. What this means is that I will invest the time to understand and review what personal and financial goals are most important to you. The benefit is I will provide a personalized analysis that aligns your goals and objectives with a plan of action."

TAKING AUTHENTIC ACTION

EXERCISE

What will you continue to do? (What is working?) _____

_____

_____

_____

What will you stop doing? (What is not working?) _____

_____

_____

_____

WHAT WILL YOU START DOING?

State one new intention _____

_____

_____

_____

Engage one new action _____

_____

_____

_____

Envision the result _____

_____

_____

_____

THE CONNECTION PRINCIPLE

Understanding and Activating the
Deep Emotions in Others

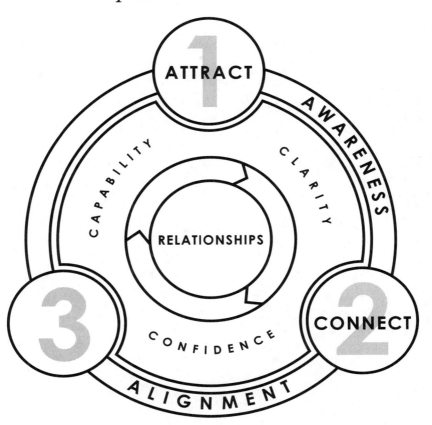

7

THE ENERGY OF RELATIONSHIPS

"Every person I have known who has been truly happy has learned how to serve others."
ALBERT SCHWEITZER

"They may forget what you said, but they will never forget how you made them feel."
CARL BUEHNER

BUILDING TO AN AUTHENTIC MINDSET

Be **clear** *love and fear are the two primary emotions that drive all behavior.*

Be **confident** *people will treat you exactly the way you ask to be treated.*

Be **capable** *of understanding and activating the deep emotions in others.*

In your life, both personally and professionally, it is not a question of whether you have relationships. The real question is, What kind of relationships do you have?

As you build to an authentic mindset and look to transition from potentially confusing your clients to connecting with them, it is important to be able to *understand and activate the deep emo-*

77

tions in others. All relationships begin with an expectation. A simple "I'll give you a call" sets an expectation that will either be met or not. Conflict and confusion occur when you say something and do not deliver on it.

> **The essence of connection:** To understand and activate the deep emotions in others.

Why do *you* act the way *you* do when *you* get upset with another person? Realize *you* had an expectation of them based on either approval or control. *You* wanted them to perform to *your* standard. When and if they did not, *your* expectation of their performance caused the problem and disconnect. Your biggest disappointments happen when you expect someone else to be, do, and act as *you* want them to. Think of how your energy is drained in these relationships.

You have experienced this professionally when someone said they would go ahead and work with you and then backed down at the eleventh hour. In your personal life, perhaps you have experienced a family member who did not deliver on a promise to pay back borrowed money, or observed a child's disappointment that his parents did not show up at his game when they said they would. How do these scenarios make you feel? These situations typically generate negative emotions such as anger, fear, shame, guilt, and apathy. *Your emotions are thoughts with feelings attached* and will manifest either negative or positive energy and actions.

Be truthful and look at your performance with your prospects and clients. Observe those situations where you created an expectation and did not deliver on it. You said one thing and did another or simply did not follow through. How, then, would you expect these prospects and clients to feel? Whose responsibility was it in the first place to create the positive energy and safe environment? You know the answers.

So many times, we show up in our prospects' lives with an expectation that they need or want our product and service without connecting to what they care about. The conversation for the most part is centered around a "me" or selling mindset versus a "we" or service mindset. Then, the professional walks away wondering why the prospect would not engage with them. What is even more compelling is that most professionals will point a finger at the prospect saying, "They were not interested." These professionals failed to recognize that when they point a finger at someone, there are three fingers pointing back at them. The truth is, they were not interesting enough to the prospect.

Human nature operates on two primary emotions: fear or love. When you choose to operate from the emotion of fear, the result is that you feel tired, alone, and negative. When you choose to operate from the emotion of love, the result is that you feel energetic, aligned with self and others, and positive.

The truth is, both of these emotions are experienced in the workplace and at home. To be able to understand the energy of these positive and negative emotions is really the essence of connecting. I don't know about you, but I'm much easier to connect with when I am putting out a positive charge to others versus a negative one. My wife and children will tell you that I am a totally different person *at home* when I am doing well *at work*.

Nationally known speaker and writer Wayne Dyer shares an interesting concept about relationships. Imagine that you have a long electrical cord hanging from your hip. With each relationship you encounter, you have the opportunity to plug into a negative source or a positive one. When you plug into negative or fear-based people, they will seem to draw all your energy from you, leaving you feeling tired and drained. When you plug into positive or love-based people, you "energize" each other and walk away feeling motivated and inspired. *You* have the choice of who you "plug into," as do your prospects and clients. The question you have to ask yourself is, Am I a source of positive or negative energy to them?

Think about your own experiences of meeting people with these two types of energy patterns. Recognize when people come into your life and are looking to take your energy. They talk poorly about others, everything seems to be "going wrong" in their life, and they have no understanding or desire to find out why. How do you feel when you are around them? These types of relationships are like trying to fit a three-pronged plug into a two-pronged outlet. The connection is not going to work unless you utilize an adapter or make an adjustment.

You also have experienced people who come into your life and make a substantial contribution. They compliment you and speak well of others. They have a great attitude and are always willing to share their positive experiences with you. You walk away from these people feeling better than before you met them.

In the initial phase of my financial career, my general agent and industry legend Al Granum had a philosophy that "people will either lift you up or beat you down." It was this philosophy that drove his recruiting process and incredible industry success. He did not let negative people into his organization who could impact the overall environment. He carefully selected who he brought in—with personality profiles, intelligence tests, etc.—to keep the culture positive and the organization a very professional and uplifting place to be. I clearly recall my initial experience of meeting Al and his associates. I could just feel the professionalism, but the most important value to me was that these associates were *likeable*.

ENERGY IN MOTION

The energy you carry, positive or negative, will show itself through your emotions. Emotions are very powerful. Break the word apart: E + Motion = energy in motion. When you say something to someone, it triggers a thought, which leads to a feeling, stirs an emotion (*a thought with a feeling attached*), and creates a decision. The thoughts will trigger logic or imagination, positive or negative emotions, and a decision that will be either yes, no, or maybe. For instance, remember the previous example about your spouse asking you to visit family when you had other plans, like watching a big sporting event with your friends, and the thoughts, feelings, and emotions this situation triggered? By the way, what did you decide to do?

Emotion: A thought with a feeling attached.

Emotions drive our decisions. In every major decision, *people buy on emotion and justify it with logic,* regardless of how conceptual or analytical they may be. Think of some of the major decisions you have made in your own life—the college you selected, buying your first new car, purchasing your dream home, and even the person you married. All were decided by emotion and justified with logic. Allow me to provide a personal example.

In 1997, I began the process of building a new home. My wife, Debbie, and children wanted me to put a pool in the backyard, but I continually resisted. My perception of a pool was that it was costly and a lot of work to maintain. It wasn't just the pool itself I objected to; there would be landscaping around the pool, a fence, and a host of other obstacles to endure. My children, who were 14, 12, and 10 at the time, would constantly bring up the subject when we visited our new home as it was being built. On many occasions, my good friend and landscape architect witnessed these discussions. He kept indicating that we had the perfect site for a pool; however, it must be installed during the construction process, not after. Getting the necessary trucks and equipment back there after we secured the property with the initial landscaping elements would be a nightmare.

I resisted for months and kept justifying to myself why we didn't need this pool. Then something happened that dramatically changed my thinking. My wife and I had dinner with two friends who were describing the happiness and joy of anticipating their daughter's wedding day. They were radiating love for their daughter and how much they were looking forward to this big day. As most men do, my friend Craig and I got around to talking about the *cost* of the big event.

He indicated that the cost would be significant. He then turned to me and with deep conviction said, "I would rather have the memory than the money."

This statement, along with his conviction about it, hit me like a sledgehammer. When you hear something that is true for you, nothing else needs to be said about it.

Shortly thereafter, my wife and I attended a function for our oldest daughter, Stefanie, who was a freshman in high school. She was competing in a national dance competition with her team. As I sat in the bleachers and watched her perform, my thoughts flashed back to when she was a baby and how she was growing up right before my eyes. I then realized I only had four years left with her in our home before she left for college, and Craig's words and meaning became resoundingly clear. I literally became emotional in the stands and, with tears in my eyes, turned to my wife and said, "I'm putting the pool in."

She looked at me a little perplexed and said, "Where did that come from?"

I reminded her of what Craig and Marilyn shared with us, and how I would like the pool to be the magnet for our children to stay home and be with us. She was obviously very pleased, and the kids were thrilled. The next day, I met with my landscape architect and told him of my decision. All of a sudden, the perceived obstacles melted away, and I was justifying to him why I *should* put the pool in. I completely reversed myself on all the elements, including the cost, saying it would be an investment in our home, I would hire a pool service, etc. The truth is, it was a great investment. We have created great memories through events centered around our backyard and pool. Our home became a haven for happy times and special events. Today, I justify my decision all the time and encourage others to "have the memory, not the money." I also can assure you that my wife reminds me of this every time she goes shopping. She will affectionately tease me and say, "I'm providing you with more memories, Hon," as she unloads her shopping bags.

LEAVE PEOPLE BETTER THAN BEFORE

As I stated before, the essence of connection is to *understand and activate the deep emotions in others.* With your understanding that 85 percent of the client creation process is based on your communication and relationship skills, keep in mind where your attention and energy have to be placed. Focus on the emotions of people and why they would do something, before telling them how to do it.

Everyone you come in contact with has different needs, wants, and values. Each of us has concerns in our lives, opportunities in front of us, and important relationships. It is important to pay attention to the *psychographics,* or perceived needs, of your prospects and clients as well as the demographics. We all enjoy talking about ourselves and want to be heard. We love to be associated with people who allow us to do this. Here is a little tip for you: *People will treat you exactly the way you ask to be treated.* If you show interest in other people's needs, wants, and values, they will find you *interesting to be with.* They will reflect back to you the very feeling you convey to them.

For example, in a recent meeting with a very successful business leader, I was reminded of the truth of this statement. I asked only four questions during the 90-minute meeting, and the person's responses engaged 75 minutes of the discussion. The bottom line is, the prospect indicated the meeting was one of the most interesting he had attended in a long time and requested a follow-up meeting as soon as possible. By conveying my interest in what he had to say, this person walked away with the feeling that I was interesting to be with.

Think beyond the obvious in order to make the connection with other people. Realize that people do things for other than apparent reasons. In many cases, people pretend to be who they are not: they may feign to know more than they do, socialize with others they really do not like, etc. While it may be obvious to you that they should make changes, they will insist on doing something their way. For example, you may have prospects who intuitively know that the suggestions you are making are valid and appropriate, but they are stuck in a negative place, because they do not know how to disengage from their current advisor. They will stay in that situation, even though they know you can help them. If you challenge the prospect on their beliefs and appear frustrated, you will always create a disconnect in that situation.

WHAT PEOPLE WANT

At times like these in your relationships, it is important to remember that everyone wants to be heard. I am reminded of that constantly as a public speaker. Each time I present to an audience, at the end of the program a select crowd always gathers around for the opportunity to talk to me. They approach me not only to say they enjoyed my words but also to tell me how it aligns with their lives and to provide personal examples. Keep this very important truth in mind: *Each and every person wants to be heard.*

GIVE PEOPLE CREDIT

President Reagan kept a plaque on his desk in the Oval Office that said, "There is no limit to what a man can do or where he can go if he doesn't mind who gets the credit." People will connect with you when you provide them with your thoughts and concepts and allow them to pass those thoughts and concepts through their filters and feed them back to you as their own. Let others manifest your ideas and own them. From an advisory point of view, you can create significant obstacles for yourself if you get hung up on owning ideas, especially with other advisors. People who share their ideas and give others credit create a positive connection in these relationships.

PEOPLE WANT TO BE ACCEPTED

The number-one need of all of us is to be accepted and loved. Our number-one fear is that of rejection and loss. To help someone understand and appreciate how to minimize their losses, while showing them how to have great gains and opportunities in their lives, is a great way to connect.

In building to an authentic mindset from a me-centered to a we-centered approach in your communications, it is important that you demonstrate compassion—to develop an understanding that everyone is doing the best they can with what they know. For example, you would not approach your teenage son regarding which mortgage program would best suit your needs to buy a new home. He likely does not have the capability to help you make such a decision. Asking this young person to provide high-level information without an understanding of the subject will potentially create stress and anxiety for him. At best, the teenager can offer an opinion. Most anyone can offer an opinion but not necessarily have enough information to make a wise decision.

The point is, most prospects do not have enough understanding of your subject matter or its nuances and do not want to admit it. Do not assume that they know something because it appears so basic to you. A great way to connect with people is to educate them with a compassionate tone: "Would it be helpful if I took time to update you on the latest developments of. . . ?" This approach conveys a feeling of empathy in that you are seeking to understand them instead of having them understand you.

When you engage people with compassion or empathy, you bring a positive energy into any discussion. By listening and being patient, you can create a safe environment for people to discuss their concerns with you. When clients feel talked down to, they feel overwhelmed, inferior, and uncomfortable with the mistakes they may have made in the past. One of the comments I received in my survey about why people will not connect with others is that they felt the communication and dialogue "made them feel stupid." Be compassionate with people and recognize we all have made decisions that have resulted in pain or dissatisfaction, disappointments or frustrations.

The opportunity before you, to understand the energy of relationships and how you can serve people, has never been more important than in our current work environment. Everyone has been set back in the past three years with the stock market and September 11. People are rethinking what matters to them. They are more open and willing to hear your ideas and suggestions. If you approach these people with a compassionate tone and remember *your emotions will be caught and not taught,* you can capture a big opportunity for yourself. With recent world events, people are changing their beliefs about their money and what they value. More important, they are looking for professionals to work with who understand who they are.

A u t h e n t i c   T r u t h s

- Emotions are caught and not taught.

- People will treat you exactly the way you ask to be treated.

- The number-one need of all of us is to be accepted and loved.

TAKING AUTHENTIC ACTION

EXERCISE

What will you continue to do? (What is working?) _____

_____

_____

_____

What will you stop doing? (What is not working?) _____

_____

_____

_____

WHAT WILL YOU START DOING?

State one new intention _____

_____

_____

_____

Engage one new action _____

_____

_____

_____

Envision the result _____

_____

_____

_____

8

THE LANGUAGE
OF TRUST

*"It takes two to speak the truth—one to speak,
and the other to listen."*
HENRY DAVID THOREAU

*"Treat people you do business with as if they were part of your
family. Prosperity depends on how much understanding one
receives and the people with whom one conducts business."*
KONOSUKE MATSUSHITA

BUILDING TO AN AUTHENTIC MINDSET

Be **clear** *it is not only what you say but also how you are saying it.*

Be **confident** *in establishing your believability in the first three minutes.*

Be **capable** *of connecting to what someone else cares about.*

In any relationship, it is not only what you say, it is *how* you say it.

Your clients are not only listening with their ears, they also are observing with their eyes. Their logical left brain is filtering your words, facts, and figures, and the right brain is reading between the lines. The right brain is observing your mannerisms, your eye contact, your tone of voice, and your demeanor and will trigger an intuitive verdict about you. This verdict, or decision, sometimes may even appear illogical. People will simply tell you, "I just have a feeling," and arrive at the conclusion they trust you or they do not.

BEHAVIOR PATTERNS

Where does trust come from? What gives you the feeling about someone that causes you to trust them or not trust them?

In his book, *You've Got to Be Believed to Be Heard* (St. Martin's, 1993), Bert Decker discusses what composes someone's *believability*. Decker cited the work of researcher Albert Mehrabian, who found that "when we send out an inconsistent message, our verbal content is usually smothered by the vocal and visual components." The results showed a whole-picture view of a typical presentation:

Verbal	7 percent
Vocal	38 percent
Visual	55 percent

I define these categories as such:

Verbal: The message itself, the words you say
Vocal: The variety, projection, and resonance of your voice
Visual: What people see, specifically in your body language

Note that what is actually being said only contributes 7 percent of a person's believability. You may feel you have the best product or service on the market, and yet you may have a total disconnect with your prospect. Your prospect does not "feel" the way you do and subsequently does not engage with you. In his book, *Storyselling for Financial Advisors,* author Mitch Anthony thoroughly addresses this language of trust.

He states, "Clients will buy inferior products from people they trust more often than they will buy superior products from people they don't trust. The ultimate consumer goal is to buy the best product from the best representative."

To better prepare yourself for your client meetings and avoid the above-mentioned scenario, it is vitally important that you develop your emotional radar as well as your intellect. The truth is, you have only one opportunity to make a good first impression. I shared with you earlier that on meeting a male prospect, he will put you through this "believability test" in 37 seconds. Women, on the other hand, will not be as generous. They will give you somewhere between 17 and 20 seconds. The true language of trust has to do with the sensory details—how you look, what you say, and how you say it. Think about speakers in the past who have engaged you. Why did you connect with them? What were they projecting to you, and how do you form your own baseline understanding of believability and trust?

THE GOLDEN RULE WITH A TWIST

One of the most effective ways to convey the language of trust is to use psychological reciprocity, or what I call the golden rule with a twist. This is simply: *Do unto others as you would have them do onto you, only do it first.* This is important in the language of trust, for it conveys *courtesy* as the attractor pattern. I based this on my experience that *what you take out of a relationship will be in proportion to what you put into it.* If I extend courtesy to people first, and they are aligned with the pattern, they oftentimes reciprocate and treat me in the same manner.

I can provide many practical examples of this powerful pattern of behavior. For example, when I initially call prospects on the phone, the first thing I say to them is, "Do you have a moment, or would there be a better time to reach you?" I recognize that a phone call is an interruption, and the prospect or client is not necessarily in a position to take my call. If they are able to speak with me, they allow me to proceed. If they are unable to do so, they let me know immediately. In either event, they get the feeling that I am being *courteous* and respectful of their time. You will be perceived as unprofessional if you proceed with trying to talk to someone when it is inappropriate to do so.

You have all received those irritating phone calls from telemarketers who mispronounce your last name and then immediately proceed to tell you why you should buy something you don't need or want. In most cases, you look for ways to disconnect from the conversation as soon as possible. The point is, you hang up on these people with a feeling that they were rude and unprofessional.

Another great application of reciprocity is the person who asks you to conduct a meeting or interview in a setting I call "out of bounds." Perhaps a prospect or client meets you in the lobby, or suggests you meet in a very noisy restaurant at the most inappropriate time. Here you are, trying to explain something very important to them, and you know you will be surrounded with distractions. When someone does this to me, I simply say, "What I would like to speak with you about is personal and confidential, and I do not feel it is appropriate to talk in this setting. May I have the courtesy of your office for five minutes please?"

If someone is aligned with the value and pattern of courtesy, they will immediately acknowledge that and say, "Of course."

If they do not, and ask you to proceed in that environment, you will have to make a choice. Remember, *people will treat you exactly the way you ask to be treated.* Be *courteous* first and expect people to respond to it.

Here is my favorite application of the power of reciprocity. I am sure you have had the experience of someone asking you to do something and then not following up with you. You may have left numerous messages for a client who refuses to return your calls. Use the concept of reciprocity to test for alignment with this person. I make one final call and ask their assistant to place me into their voice mail, and I leave the following reply: "John, you have asked me to do some work on your behalf, and I followed through on that request. I have left you numerous messages to provide you with this information, and I would really appreciate the *courtesy* of a return phone call."

And then I hang up. I say no more and no less.

Experience this for yourself and see what kind of results you obtain. I have had people call me at home in the evening, call me while they were on airplanes, call from vacation, and numerous other scenarios to return my call. These prospects and clients are totally aligned with the pattern of *courtesy*.

On the other hand, I have had several instances over the past 27 years where people did not return my phone call. Based on this principle, I am comfortable with the fact that they do not align with courtesy. Therefore, I make a business decision and decide right there and then to disengage from the relationship. I am no longer interested in extending my services to anyone who would ask me to operate outside of my level of integrity.

THE FIRST 30 SECONDS

The most important element you can develop to communicate the language of trust to someone happens in the first 30 seconds of your presentation. Whether you believe it or not, your prospects will form a perception about you when they first meet you. The next 30 seconds will either confirm or deny their findings. I will share my opening statement with you and then provide the thought process behind it.

Thank you for choosing to meet with me today. I know your time, like mine, is valuable, and I will focus on making this meeting as effective as I can. As you know, we were introduced by _____. He spoke highly of you and made no assumptions that you would require my services. As I promised, my intention for today is to invest the time required to get to know you and what you care about, share who I am, describe how I serve, and then I will leave. We will then decide together how I can be of service to you. Fair enough?

My intention with this statement is to establish believability and trust. It has three vital components:

1. You are extending courtesy to the prospect by thanking him and acknowledging that he made a choice to visit with you. You did not force yourself on him and into this potential relationship. It was his choice, and you appreciate and respect it.

2. You connect to his trust filter by reminding him how you were introduced through someone of whom he thinks highly. The best form of establishing this initial contact is by way of an introduction from someone esteemed in that person's peer group. You can *borrow* the trust of someone else until you establish it yourself.

3. You are making no expectations that the prospect wants to go any further. Therefore, he will not feel a sense of obligation or fear that you will try to sell him anything he does not want or need. The only decision the prospect has to make now is whether or not he wants to engage with you.

Keep in mind the other subtle facts that go along with this critical first 30 seconds. How do you look, how do you shake someone's hand, do you have eye contact, are you dressed appropriately, and, above all, do you pronounce the person's name correctly? All these little things send a signal to your prospect's emotional radar. Remember, 93 percent of your believability is attributed to your vocal and visual impact. Your door of opportunity will open or close to the extent you pay attention to these vital elements.

THE FIRST THREE MINUTES

If the first 30 seconds establishes your believability, the first three minutes establishes your credibility. Once you establish your intention for the meeting, the client's emotional radar is checking to see if there are any bogies in your presentation. I encourage you to internalize and master your first three minutes rather than simply memorize and potentially sound canned. When you incorporate elements in your presentation that you are clear and confident about, and play to your strengths, you will develop a superbly mastered approach. The following elements are what I include in my first three minutes:

- A Reciprocity Statement (the first 30 seconds)
- Personal Value Statement
- Company Value Statement
- Process Value Statement
- CORE Statements—How you serve others
- Trust Factor Question

In Chapter 6, I addressed the importance and template for building out powerful value statements. Take the time to build these out and make them compelling. They are vitally important in your approach. Do not discount the believability and credibility factor that these statements will provide for you.

The CORE statements, which we will build out in greater detail in Chapter 9, are utilized to let the prospect know how you have served others effectively. CORE is an acronym that allows you to briefly provide an overview of how you have helped other people with their *concerns, opportunities,* important *relationships,* and your *experience.*

I addressed clients' CORE issues by stating how I help other professionals eliminate *concerns* and realize new *opportunities.* I briefly state how I provide introductions to strategic *relationships* and then share an overview of my *experience.* The opportunity before you is to tailor the discussion to specific discussion points that are relevant to the prospect and not yourself.

These elements should take no more than three minutes to deliver.

THE TRUST FACTOR QUESTION

This is the most important component of the first three minutes. Your intention at this critical point is to test for alignment with what you have previously stated. You should be conscious of prospects' emotional radar and shift all focus from yourself to them. It is at this time I ask a provocative, probing question that implies I am there to serve and not sell them.

My intention is to engage in a conversation and not make a formal presentation. I choose to guide the discussion but not control the content. I am looking to discern if the client *trusts* me enough to go forward with the discussion. My Trust Factor Question is:

> What is it that you care about that, if I were able to help you focus on and accomplish in the next 12 months, would make you feel happy with your progress, both personally and professionally?

The purpose of this question is to help me establish as quickly as possible what I call the *dominant emotional reason*. My intent is to focus on what prospects feel is the most important issue in their life at this time. I already know why I am there, so there is no reason in my mind to continue to overwhelm the prospect with frivolous or unnecessary communication. I do not have preconceived notions, and I allow the client to set the agenda for the meeting. In my experience, if prospects will answer the Trust Factor Question, we are initially in alignment and have a green light to proceed. More important, uncovering this dominant emotional reason and centering the discussion around it will dramatically up the odds of connecting. You have a 70 percent chance of converting prospects to clients once they answer this question.

Dominant emotional reason: The number-one emotional reason that causes a person to act.

THE BENEFITS OF THE QUESTION

The use of this question can help you create a shift in the mind of the prospect. Katherine F., financial representative, shared with me that before learning the Trust Factor Question, it was hard for her to position asking clients about their long-term and short-term planning objectives without the question sounding somewhat negative, more specifically, alluding to the fact that the client has done insufficient planning to this point. The Trust Factor Question has helped her to focus on progress with her client, which is positive, versus regress with her client, which is negative.

What it can mean to you is the client perceives you more as an advisor and confidant versus a salesperson. The real benefit is that a client aligns with your *we*-centered approach versus a *me*-centered approach. In addition, there are three extremely powerful benefits by using this question:

1. *The willingness to answer the question indicates whether or not a client trusts you.* The very way in which the question is framed focuses the client's attention over the next 12 months. More important, you refer directly to how you can help this person connect with what they believe is important. The fact that they respond at all indicates they see you in this role as serving and helping accomplish what they deeply care about. You are presenting yourself as the person who could help them focus on and accomplish the most important issue in their life at this time.

2. *Asking a direct question elicits a truthful response.* When you ask the Trust Factor Question, people will initially break eye contact with you and go into their right brain, which will cause them to think in futuristic terms. In my experience, they almost always tell me the truth about what is important to them. This is not something they choose to fabricate, embellish, or lie about. They tend to tell me what's in their hearts right now. My solutions can only be effective when I receive information that is truthful and useful. The answers allow you to get right to the emotional blueprint of prospects and focus on their most significant issues. Most important, prospects will lead you to the very subject that they want to talk about.

3. *When people communicate what they care about, it places you in a position to serve them, either through direct action or by referring them to someone in your network.* In my experience, some of the largest cases I have ever developed were not initially within my core competency. For example, people have responded to the Trust Factor Question by indicating that the most important issue in their life is resolution with a spouse. In that situation, I recognized the prospect would not do any real planning without first resolving this important issue. If I ignored it and simply set it aside, they would get the feeling the conversation was about me and not about them, and a disconnect would occur. In these situations, I would offer my services to refer to outside experts whose knowledge may serve them at this time. Most prospects are simply amazed with this attitude of service.

I have recommended specialists in all areas with many prospects and clients. It continually sends the message that I am there to serve in any way that I can. By putting their best interests ahead of my own in these situations, I have been rewarded many times over. I may not initially get the "result," but what goes around comes around. Sooner or later, I am "paid," either directly or with a strong introduction to someone else.

Let me provide you with a synchronistic example of how this service mindset can benefit you. I met with a prospect named John and asked him the Trust Factor Question. He answered that he really wanted to retire and enjoy his true love, which was airplanes. He really was not in the position to do significant planning until he sold his business. Recognizing I couldn't really provide him with any service until then, I offered an introduction to an investment banker. He readily accepted and, within a short time, began the process of working with this specialist on promoting the sale of his business. He called to thank me for the introduction and said he would stay in touch with me.

Nearly three months later, I met with Steve and asked him the Trust Factor Question. Steve's biggest concern was a family property he had inherited from his father's estate for which he could not find a buyer. That property was zoned as a single-use item as a municipal airport. While the land was valuable, it had to remain an airport, and Steve had difficulty finding anyone who was interested in the property. I recalled my conversation with John and put the two of them together. During this period of time, John had received an offer on his business. With the current opportunity in front of him, John took the offer and proceeded to work out an arrangement to purchase Steve's property. I was able to help them both accomplish what they cared about and what was most important to them.

The benefit to me was the fact that they both immediately contacted me at separate times to utilize my services. I helped Steve with his newfound liquidity with estate and retirement planning, and I helped John with the necessary planning for his new business interest. The most important thing to note was that they both had existing advisors prior to meeting me. They both engaged me for my services and did not even consider their existing relationships. By showing the attitude of service and focusing on their most important issue, I was rewarded with not only substantial commissions but also two quality client relationships, which I still maintain today.

Paying attention to what makes you believable will go a long way in helping you project the language of trust. By engaging with empathy and reciprocity and engaging the Trust Factor Question, you will develop three green lights to proceed with your prospects and clients.

A*uthentic* **T***ruths*

- Your believability is established in the first 30 seconds.

- Do unto others as you would have them do unto you, only do it first.

- What you take from a relationship will be in direct proportion to what you put into it.

YOUR TOUGH QUESTIONS

EXERCISE

The Trust™ Question
"What is it that you deeply care about, that if you were able to accomplish it in the next year, would make you feel happy with your progress both personally and professionally?

If the process you are currently using in your business were to be the process for all of us to follow, would you change anything?

If the way you were acting in relationships was to be the model for us all to follow, would you act differently?

9

THE ELEMENTS OF A CARING CONVERSATION

"Questions are the creative acts of intelligence."
FRANK KING

"Sometimes you have to be silent in order to be heard."
WILMA ASKINAS

BUILDING TO AN AUTHENTIC MINDSET

Be **clear** that people assess your professionalism and knowledge by the questions you ask.

Be **confident** in your ability to listen.

Be **capable** of having a conversation that replaces complexity with intimacy.

In a survey reported by *USA Today,* 3,500 CEOs, men and women alike from a cross section of industries, were asked how they assess the professionalism and knowledge of financial advisors. There was one resoundingly consistent answer, one that most professionals might be surprised to hear. The answer given by an overwhelming majority was also the factor that most influenced the decision to work with this advisor. The answer was, "The kinds of questions they ask me." Think of how compelling this information really is to your success. Far too many professionals act unconsciously in their meetings, asking irrelevant or leading questions without paying attention to their implications. Many professionals are simply afraid to ask tough questions for fear that the client may get upset with them. The ultimate irony is the questions you avoid asking are the very questions that your prospects and clients would like you to ask them.

Asking intelligent questions can be the most profound method of persuasion you will ever utilize. Professionals who develop the skill of asking intelligent, incisive, probing questions also possess superior skills in giving intelligent answers. However, I have observed that the opposite is not always true. I have known many professionals who can give intelligent answers but quite often are not very effective at asking good questions, or worse, ask no questions at all.

THE POWER OF A QUESTION

As I cited in the opening attribution, "Questions are the creative acts of intelligence." Most prospects and clients who you encounter certainly have problems. A profound truth is that *the problem is rarely the problem and the solution is rarely the solution.* The real problem is they don't know how to think about their problem. Good questions can clear the fog and help someone see what the real issues are.

A good question provides a transformative experience for your prospects and clients. When you ask a question such as the Trust Factor Question, you allow prospects to get outside of their own way of thinking. It is the question that stimulates the experience, not the answer. The question is the key that unlocks the door to transforming the prospect's problem into an opportunity. The point is, *how they think about their problem is 50 percent of the solution.*

I have witnessed this many times with the answers I have received with the Trust Factor Question. People may have been thinking about the issue internally, but until the question is directly asked of them, their answers are irrelevant. I have experienced firsthand, when asking prospects what they care about or want to focus on at this time in their life, that the answers come in rapid-fire succession. Simply asking "Is there anything else?" often unleashes a torrent of issues that they have been internalizing but have never expressed.

In all of your prospect and client meetings, you ask questions, but what is more important is the *kind* of questions you ask. As you transition from the me-centered or selling mindset to the we-centered or serving mindset, you will gradually apply more probing versus prompting questions. The exercises I have given you throughout this book are probing questions. They are tough questions, questions only you can answer. Ask yourself the following question, "What is it that I care about, that if I focus on and accomplish in the next 12 months will make me feel happy with my progress personally and professionally?" It is through the question itself that you will transform your experience of yourself to your career.

Jake C., financial representative, asked himself this question when he had a tough decision to make about whether to stay in his current career or choose another. The clarity that he got from answering the Trust Factor Question had a great impact on his ability to make his decision. He then had the confidence to implement the use of the question in all of his client meetings over the next quarter. To this single question he attributed over $50,000 in income, giving him one of his strongest quarters ever.

> A tough question is honest, truthful, asks for something you do not know, and does not set conditions for a response, but merely asks what the response should be.

You have undoubtedly been in the presence of people who have responded, "That is a great question." You have stimulated their thinking in a way that allows them to think about the problem from a different perspective. Many people have reported back to me after using the Trust Factor Question in their meetings, they have opened cases with existing clients that they would never have thought about. The question opened the client's mind, and the professional could add value through experience and strategic relationships that elevated their stature in the eyes of the client.

Let me share with you another story that illustrates the benefit of using the Trust Factor Question. Britt Y., a veteran financial services representative, was putting together group plans for an organization of 40 people and had already secured the accounts. Part of completing the process was establishing a pretax insurance plan. This could have been seen as a formality and not really given additional effort, because he had already sold what he was brought in to do. Britt knew, however, that his opportunities had just begun. He sat down with one of the individuals, proceeded with his approach, and completed it by asking the Trust Factor Question. By asking this question, Britt was able to find out that this client did trust him and that the dominant emotional reason this prospect would move forward was to ease his wife's fear of unforeseen disasters and circumstances. By asking the Trust Factor Question, Britt was able to connect this gentleman's love for his wife by alleviating her greatest fear, as well as produce another $15,000 in income through other services he provided.

A probing question is asked to acquire information. When you ask prospects probing questions, you are seeking to understand them. You would like to learn more about their attitudes, motives, values, feelings, etc. The Trust Factor Question is a probing question. A prompting question, on the other hand, is asked when *you* seek to be understood. You want to know if the prospect or client is likely to do something. You are attempting to direct or lead the prospect. An example of a prompting question is, "If I could show you a way to save time and money, would you be interested?" These prompting or leading questions are typical in the sales profession. Both types of questions have their place; however, I think you can see how the prospect or client may know where you are going with a prompting technique, may resist, and, ultimately, may disconnect.

I recently had this kind of experience while shopping for a car with my daughter. The salesman was asking a series of prompting questions in a very irritating manner. He finished his mediocre approach by asking the question, "If I can give you the right price, will you buy a car today?"

My daughter, who is only 20, looked at him and said, "I really would like to drive the car first before I make a decision."

This sad but true demonstration of how people attempt to connect with each other should remind you that *answers are only important when you ask the right question.* I have observed some initial training that suggests the first question you should ask is, "What is the proper spelling of your last name?" Think about how this prospect would feel about you, your knowledge, and professionalism with this leading question. What would you think about this professional?

There is a humorous example of this in the movie *The Pink Panther Strikes Again,* starring the late Peter Sellers as Inspector Clouseau. In the scene, Clouseau asks an old man sitting next to a dog, "Does your dog bite?"

The man replies, "No."

When Clouseau leans down to pet it, the dog nearly rips his hand off.

"I thought you said your dog doesn't bite?" says Clouseau.

"That," said the old man, "is not my dog."

Once again, the answer is only important when you ask the right question.

THE POWER OF LISTENING

It is one thing to be able to ask intelligent questions, and it is another thing to be able to listen to the answers. I have been in countless meetings and observed the following: *While many profes-*

sionals have talked their way out of a sale, nobody ever "listened" them-selves out of one. You most likely have experienced someone asking you a question and cutting you off as you began to answer. How did this make you feel? Remember, people want to be heard, and the best way to elevate your status from *salesperson to confidant* is to let your prospect or client finish talking. Additional benefits of listening are:

- It shows respect.
- It establishes trust.
- It increases knowledge.
- It generates ideas.
- It creates loyalty.

When you listen, you seek to better understand your prospects or clients. There is a big difference between hearing and listening to someone. When you are hearing them, you are merely waiting for your turn to speak your mind and listening only for the information that applies to what you want to talk about.

Those who listen are looking to learn about the experiences and views of their clients. By doing so, the client reciprocates and gives your answers more credibility. If you are doing all the talking, how will you ever learn about what the client thinks and feels? If you are doing all the talking versus listening, you have no way of telling what the client is looking for. You have two ears and one mouth. If you remind yourself of this simple truth and spend two-thirds of your time listening, and one-third of your time talking, you will dramatically increase your effectiveness to connect.

HAVING A CARING CONVERSATION

One of the most important things you can learn to do is set up an environment where people can be safe in sharing their personal stories and visions and have a caring conversation. I am very comfortable in sharing with prospects or clients that I prefer to have a conversation with them and not make a presentation. I also ask if we can have this meeting in a place of truth. A caring conversation in the authentic mindset has the following elements:

- **A caring conversation is personalized, not generalized.** I prefer to talk *to* prospects, not *at* prospects. I pace my conversation at their level of understanding about something, not mine. I will do my homework about them and research their industry. My intention is to project that this meeting is important and that the discussion is centered around them.
- **Provide information and not advice.** Advice tends to be perceived as "telling me what to do." No one likes to be told what to do. I simply present information through the filter of what it could mean to them and how they can benefit from something. I then will leave it up to them to determine if it is important or not. Ultimately, I get their feedback and direction on the information, which can then be positioned in a quality solution.
- **Replace complexity with intimacy.** I will relate to prospects' motives, feelings, and personalities by asking probing questions. My intention is to learn about them, what makes them tick, and to uncover the dominant emotional reason they will do anything with anybody.
- **Replace confusion with clarity.** Remember the power of your words. Each word can impact the outcome of the situation; each word can make a difference. I focus on telling the prospect what something does and not what it is. Our subject matter is confusing enough, and too many times we use industry jargon and speak right over the heads of our prospects and clients.

I am reminded of this last point on a regular basis. Recently, I wanted to expand my Web site capability and had a meeting with a technical consultant. He presented himself in such a manner that I understood very little. He used technical terms, hid behind his laptop, never made eye contact with me, and, more important, never asked me any probing questions. When he finished presenting, he asked me for a decision. I responded, "I have to think about it." The truth was, I didn't understand anything he said.

In Chapter 8, I talked about the importance of obtaining the dominant emotional reason from the client, which is the number-one reason they will do anything with anybody. The Trust Factor Question helps secure this response. I always set up this question by saying: "I do not want to make any assumptions on how I may serve you. Would it be okay with you if I start this meeting by getting your answer to one question to help set the agenda for today?" I then ask the Trust Factor Question, which is, "What is it that you deeply care about that, if I were able to help you focus on and accomplish in the next 12 months, would make you happy with your progress, both personally and professionally?"

The key point is, I have learned that if you ask clients' permission to ask them what you feel is a compelling or provocative question and they respond favorably, you can ask them anything. This is an important concept to understand. When you feel you are about to ask a tough question, simply ask prospects for their approval. You may suggest, "This question may be difficult to ask, but I feel it is appropriate to our discussion. Would it be okay if I asked you?" By using this reciprocity statement, you open the door to a caring conversation.

For example, I was introduced by a very good client to a prospect who was very successful but having marital difficulties. I knew this would impact the prospect's ability to do any planning. After asking the Trust Factor Question, I asked his permission to ask him a sensitive question. He agreed, and I asked him about his relationship with his wife. He became very emotional and spoke freely and openly about his relationship. He later commented on my courage to bring it up and understood how important this issue was to his future and his planning.

Once clients agree to answer the Trust Factor Question and provide you with an answer, you are in the position to remove your selling hat and get into the role of serving them. Prospects will tell you things they have never told anyone else. Don't be surprised if they freely admit this to you after the conversation. It is one of the greatest compliments a client can give, as it confirms that they trust you and that you have asked meaningful questions. If you keep the conversation centered around what they want to talk about—and their agenda not yours—you will create alignment and trust.

The CORE conversation is focused around the response to the Trust Factor Question. Once you have this answer from the client, the conversation is then centered around:

- **Challenges.** What would keep this from happening? What obstacles are in the way? What are your biggest concerns right now? Your intent is to eliminate potential dangers for the prospect.
- **Opportunities.** What are your prospects excited about? How can you help them capture these opportunities?
- **Relationships.** Who are the people who are most influential in their life personally and professionally? What relationships can you provide to prospects to enhance the quality of their lives?
- **Experiences.** Reinforce and maximize prospects' strengths. Talk about what is working and not working for them. Share your knowledge and experience with them, and how you have helped others in similar situations.

Centering your discussion around the client's CORE issues allows you to have a caring and courageous conversation. More important, this format allows you to engage with people regardless of their personality style. You may have a prospect who is very conceptual or very analytical. By keeping your conversation focused on the CORE issues of the prospect, you can be effective with all types of prospects.

Brian S., a financial representative with two years of experience, was looking to align with organizations in his community where he could share his financial services skills. Brian located an organization near him that would give him this opportunity. One of the concerns Brian had going into his first meeting was that he was young, new to the industry, and he questioned what kind of value he could bring. He thought he would go to just listen and observe to see if it was something he could feel good about joining. One of the drivers for Brian in his business was to be a well-respected professional, so that he could walk down the hall of his office and be recognized for the value he brought. This intention remained with him as he entered the conference center for his first meeting. His concern manifested quickly when everyone he saw was twice his age. He took a seat and listened to many speakers talk about many different topics and agendas. The more he heard, the more he noticed that the organization had no clear intention and, therefore, was spinning its wheels, yielding to the egos of its members. Later in the meeting, individuals were given the opportunity to stand up and introduce themselves to the current members. Brian stood up and gave his Personal Value Statement with complete confidence and then followed up with a question that caught everybody by surprise. He asked, "What is it that the members of this organization care about that, if they were able to focus on and accomplish in the next 12 months, would make them feel happy with their progress?"

He then proceeded to say that it was clear that everyone could communicate the concerns of the Board, but what were their opportunities, who were the people they wanted to have an impact on, and which were the current relationships that could help. Finally, he asked them what kind of experience they would like to have being a member of this organization. Brian walked an entire organization through the CORE conversation and was not only welcomed in but also elected as the youngest member to the Board.

Think of how this would be applied in your own life. If your number-one issue professionally were to obtain better quality prospects to talk with, how would you feel about someone who could help you remove the obstacles that were keeping this from happening? Someone who could help you capture the opportunity to engage new clients who are leaving other advisors? Someone who could enhance the quality of your life by making strategic introductions? Someone who could keep you focused and confident, using your strengths on a regular basis. Would you feel this person would be valuable in your life?

I utilize the CORE conversation with everyone in my life. I engage my children by asking them what is the most important thing happening in their lives at this time? When they respond, we talk about their challenges, opportunities, and important people in their lives, and what they are learning from their experience. It creates stimulating conversation, and, more important, I connect with my kids, and they have the feeling I am interested in their lives.

It is a sad but true fact that people in America today watch approximately 33 hours of television per week, spend three to four hours a day behind a computer, and yet spend less than five minutes a day in intimate conversation with the people they love.

In my experience, when you can help people identify their dominant emotional reason and align it with a CORE conversation, you will make a great impact with them. What this means is that you elevate your status in the eyes of your prospects and clients. The benefit is that you will develop a sustaining and significant relationship with them.

A*u t h e n t i c* **T***r u t h s*

- The problem is rarely the problem, and the solution is rarely the solution.

- Answers are only important when you ask the right questions.

- You may talk yourself out of a sale, but you will never "listen" yourself out of a sale.

THE CORE™ WORKSHEET

TOOL

The Trust Factor Question

What is it that you care about, that if I were to help you focus on and accomplish in the next 12 months, would make you happy with your progress, both personally and professionally?

Personal: _____

_____

_____

_____

_____

_____

	The CORE™ Questions	Sample Questions	
CLIENT	**CONCERNS:** −Challenges −Obstacles −Risks		Priority
CLIENT	**OPPORTUNITIES:** −Yourself −Your business −Your process		Priority
CLIENT — YOU	**RELATIONSHIPS:** −How others describe you −Reasons people associate with you −Values/Qualities that attract you to others		Priority
CLIENT — YOU	**EXPERIENCE:** −Things that make you tick −Things that people can count on from you −Things you really love to do		Priority

THE CORE™ WORKSHEET

TOOL _____

Professional: _____

_____

_____

_____

_____

_____

_____

_____

_____

Personal		Professional	
	Priority		Priority
	Priority		Priority
	Priority		Priority
	Priority		Priority

10

IDENTIFYING YOUR REAL PRODUCTS

"Service is the rent each of us pays for living–the very purpose of life and not something you do in your spare time or after you have reached your personal goals."
MARIAN WRIGHT EDELMAN

"Everyone can be great because everyone can serve."
MARTIN LUTHER KING, JR.

BUILDING TO AN AUTHENTIC MINDSET

Be **clear** *people love being served but dislike being sold.*

Be **confident** *your process of relating to others is your real product.*

Be **capable** *of anticipating your clients' needs before they ask.*

As you might imagine, my work requires a modest amount of travel between my speeches and workshops. Several years ago, I was working heavily in the St. Louis area with a major client and a workshop series. My client recommended that I stay at the Ritz-Carlton Hotel, and my assistant made the arrangements. The rest, as they say, is history. After six months of visiting St. Louis regularly, it became a ritual for me to stay at the Ritz. As my taxi pulled up, Delman, the doorman, would greet me with a friendly, "Welcome back, Mr. Cassara." The concierge would stop what she was doing and call me by name, and I knew most of the staff personally. At check-in, there would be a personal note from the hotel manager welcoming me back. I was often given an upgraded room without even asking for it. Inside the room would be a fruit basket or a glass of cognac. The food was superb, and the room service was incredible. There were times it seemed I had just hung up the phone and there would be a knock on the door. They truly were acting on their credo, "Ladies and gentlemen, serving ladies and gentlemen." From my perspective, the value of their service and the experience they provided far outweighed the cost of the room.

WHAT MAKES THE DIFFERENCE

It can't be said enough that *people love being served but dislike being sold.* Service is a powerful attractor pattern, where selling is a negative one. Service is like flowing with the current, and selling is like paddling as hard as you can upstream. The difference is all in how you relate to someone. The clue is in the word relationships. *It is your process of relating to others that is your real product.*

THE REAL PRODUCT

I often ask professionals what are their products and the benefits they offer, and they almost always immediately default to the obvious. Consistently, their answers are a list of services—life insurance, disability insurance, long-term care, group health, wills and trusts, tax returns, etc. I remind them at that time what a great opportunity they have to really think through what their real product is. In many cases, I provide a hint to them, that *people exchange a check for a feeling.* Knowing your real value and being able to distinguish how you are different from someone else is the first step in communicating it. It is your responsibility to demonstrate how you and your process make *you* different and unique. There are a lot of other professionals who provide similar services, so the question is, What sets you apart? How do you answer the question when your prospect asks: "I am currently working with someone who provides similar services. What makes you different?" You may have heard, "Aren't all companies and products the same?"

Bill D., an attorney, cited in a recent workshop that his real product was his integrity. He proclaimed to all of us that his documents are *free* and that what the client pays him for are his knowledge and wisdom. It is interesting to note that he is one of the most successful attorneys in the Chicago area.

Be truthful in how you respond to these probing questions. Keep this very compelling truth in mind: *In order for clients to engage your services, they have to fire someone else.* If prospects feel there is no added value or difference in you or your service, they will simply stay with the incumbent. Let's look at the real product of some great companies. What causes people to buy from Nordstrom rather than a discount chain? Why do I prefer to stay at a Ritz-Carlton instead of a roadside motel? Why is Southwest Airlines the fastest growing and most profitable airline in the country? What are certain companies providing that compels consumers to write checks to them? After all, clothes are clothes, a bed is a bed, an airline is an airline. The golden answer is *service.*

People write big checks to be served but will discount the purchase of a commodity. A classic example of this is the average family's trip to Disney World. They have no problem paying the admission fee at the park, paying top dollar for accommodations on the grounds, paying $15 for a hamburger, or paying $30 for a picture of their kids with Mickey Mouse. At the same time, they will spend hours online trying to find a discounted flight and car rental to get their family to Orlando and to the park. They do this because they are willing to pay top dollar for the *experience.* Herein lies the great secret of service: Make your process of relating to your clients an experience they won't forget.

Walt Disney was a great visionary. He lived by the words, "You will have unlimited abundance when you do what you do so well, that when others see what it is that you do, they will want to see it again, and they will bring others with them to see what it is that you do."

Imagine your practice where people are attracted to you because you engage them empathetically, make a positive contribution to their life, help them see their vision, and empower them to act on it. What would that mean to you personally and professionally?

Experiences can be defined as all that is perceived, remembered, and understood. Based on this definition, it is important to pay attention to both positive and negative experiences. It is clearly your responsibility to provide a good experience to your prospects and clients. Your process of relating to others is your unique way of making the difference.

HOW DECISIONS GET MADE

By now, I trust I have made it very clear that *people exchange a check for a feeling.* As you present your information, it triggers thoughts, which stir emotions and lead to decisions. If you focus your communication around the commodity and stay logical with your approach, you will get one result. If you focus on values and experiences in your communication, you will obtain another. The first step in creating your experience is to identify your real products as the feelings and emotions you want your prospects and clients to experience.

With that understanding, your real products in the financial services industry are centered around certain feelings, which include happiness, peace of mind, significance, security, confidence, comfort, harmony, joy, service, freedom, simplicity, respect, etc. I have never met anyone who wanted to buy life insurance, but I have met many people who wanted a feeling of security, comfort, and peace of mind. Prospects and clients do not write checks to save for a college education, but they do write checks for the feeling of being a good provider to their children. So many times, professionals forget this important point and focus their discussion around the commodity of *insurance* and avoid engaging the feelings.

The second step to creating a unique experience will be to identify the *real benefits* you offer. Remember, you are looking to address the question, "Why should I leave my current advisor and work with you?" How do you distinguish yourself from your competition? How do you communicate the value you will bring to someone else? The answers to these questions are critical to your success. Whether you pay attention to it or not, *the value your clients place on you is in direct proportion to the size of the check they write for your services.* If they write you a small check for term insurance and give the big investment check to someone else, that is their way of reflecting their perceived value of you.

Your actions speak volumes about your own beliefs and about how you add value to others. In Part I, I mentioned how important it is for you to own the products and services that you are asking someone else to consider. You simply cannot be effective with anyone else if you yourself have not made the commitment to understand what it takes to do what you are asking someone else to do. You will continually get "knocked off center" and look very foolish. You will not be able to elevate yourself to a higher level of prospect or client without talking about your service from your own experience. To effectively answer the questions raised above, your prospects are looking for specific actions you can demonstrate that will provide results they don't already have. If you focus your response around these three points, you can build an effective and engaging answer to how you could make a difference:

1. Leadership
2. Relationships
3. Creativity

The primary benefit or action that can set you apart is your *leadership* skills. Share with your prospects and clients how you can help them with their biggest challenges and keep them out of danger. Share your experiences with them on how you have provided other clients with opportunities that they never knew existed before they met you. Bring these two things to your prospects and clients, and you will be valuable to them.

The second benefit or action you can provide to your clients is introductions to *strategic relationships*. Tell prospects that you have built an extensive network of professionals who can serve them for their various planning requirements. If you don't have this network, create it, because this is a valuable service to offer other people. I shared with you my own experiences of success in making strategic introductions to people outside of my core competency. This has produced great success for me in my career. Take the time to align yourself with others who have unique talents that you do not have.

The third benefit or action you provide is your *creativity* in how you communicate to your clients. Perhaps you have a unique proposal and tools that make your information easier to understand and that create a positive experience. If you do not have something in place, align yourself with people in the industry who have produced effective and innovative delivery systems. Be creative with your ideas, for it is another truth *that ideas can be sold where products cannot.* You can be extremely valuable to another person if you are known as a person who consistently comes up with great ideas.

CLARITY IS THE FIRST STEP
TOWARD MASTERY

In my own practice over the years, I have consistently aligned myself with great talent who would enhance my strengths. In my model of *Attract, Connect, and Commit,* I recognized the unique skills and abilities necessary in each area of the process. I would focus on the attraction elements, the discovery process, and the marketing. My late partner, Alan Salus, would help in the connection elements, design the proposal, and get involved in the meetings. Our third strategic partner, Ira Neiman, the attorney, would implement the strategies through legal documents and by helping us fulfill and maintain the commitment. If any of us were re-aligned in our process, we would have a totally different result. By focusing on our strengths and the right part of the process, we created a very unique and valuable experience for the clients we served over the years.

Attract	Why	Marketing
Connect	What	Selling
Commit	How	Serving

By taking the time to examine your process and understand what your real products and benefits are, you will be able to *anticipate your clients' needs before they ask.* Take the time to work *on* your business and not *in* it. Assemble your dream team, examine your marketing materials, and, above all, be capable of communicating your real value to your prospects and clients.

A u t h e n t i c   T r u t h s

- People exchange a check for a feeling.

- People will write a large check to be served but will discount the price of a commodity.

- Ideas can be sold where products cannot.

KNOW YOUR "REAL VALUE"

EXERCISE

What are your "real products"?

What are the "real benefits"?

11

SAYING WHAT YOU MEAN, MEANING WHAT YOU SAY

"An honest man's word is as good as his bond."
HENRY DAVID THOREAU

"A thought which does not result in an action is nothing much, and an action which does not proceed from a thought is nothing at all."
GEORGES BERNANOS

BUILDING TO AN AUTHENTIC MINDSET

Be **clear** *people hear and incorporate only what they understand.*

Be **confident** *in converting information to compelling statements.*

Be **capable** *of communicating clearly, effectively, and with purpose.*

I have been in many meetings in my career where multiple advisors have been seated around the table along with the client. After the meeting, I always established a policy of debriefing everyone and getting viewpoints and feedback. Here we had four experts in their fields: the attorney, the CPA, the investment advisor, and myself as the insurance specialist. As I went around the table and asked for input, the attorney said the meeting was productive, the CPA felt we did not get enough details, the investment advisor was frustrated, and I thought we connected to what mattered most to the client. Four different professionals had four different perspectives on what just happened.

This is so often the case in our prospect and client meetings. We, as professionals, may think the conflict occurs in these relationships when we cannot get the client to agree on a solution or direction. The real issue, as in the scenario I described above, is that most people cannot agree on what happened. We all have a different level of understanding on what we see, hear, and experience. The content we discussed is perceived through different contextual understandings.

The content of your presentation represents the words you say. The contextual understanding is how someone perceives it. It is like asking various people to define the word *success.* If you ask five different people, you will get five different answers. The lesson here is that *people hear and incorporate only what they understand.* In every interaction, you have the opportunity to create clarity or confusion. You can talk to their left brain with facts and figures, or you can speak to their intuitive right brain with terms of values and benefits. The point is, we must do both to create an effective presentation and good communication.

Facts stated by themselves are like onions: they don't taste good by themselves. People need the connection to the right brain by sharing what something means to them, and how they can benefit from what you just said. In every meeting, you must present your information in a way that it passes through your prospect's personality and VCR filter. Whenever you simply state a fact and leave it at that, you leave it completely up to prospects to decide based on what they *believe* rather than on what they were *told.*

An example of this is stating a claim or *fact* to your client that *your* company is the best in the industry. Whenever you state a fact all by itself and do not conclude the thought, people tend to dismiss it. By passing the fact through their filter, people can draw their own conclusion, and if they believe it, they will align with yours. Otherwise, they might say to themselves, "Everybody tells me the same thing."

Perhaps you have had a similar experience to mine purchasing a computer. I made the mistake of getting on the phone with one of those world-class techies who only spoke computerese. In the first few minutes, all I heard was bits, bytes, RAM, ISPs, html, gigabytes, etc. I finally had to stop the person and ask him, "What does all that mean to me?" He then explained something about memory. I finally asked him, "How can I benefit from one computer versus another?" His answer was nebulous at best, and I ended up telling him I had to go and hung up. I am a much more conceptual versus analytical person. I understood very little of what he said and therefore chose not to listen and not purchase his computer system. I continued my search until I finally met the person who could answer my questions. This person communicated effectively at my level of understanding and received my business. Don't get me wrong, I love computers—they help me solve problems I never had before.

The point here is, you cannot simply speak facts to your prospects and clients and be effective. You must take the time to convert your factual points and data into compelling statements that appeal to their understanding. Be truthful—you know the average consumer has a perception that financial planning is complicated. Consumers especially feel this way about estate planning and legal work. To the extent that you pay attention and convert your facts to compelling statements, you will find yourself connecting more effectively.

CONVERTING FACTS TO COMPELLING STATEMENTS

One of the truths I have observed about experienced professionals is that the longer they are in their career, the less they seem to pay attention to the nuances of their communication skills. Along with their success, they have developed good habits as well as bad ones. The good news is, they have established their competency, a client base, and a long list of initials after their names. The bad news is that they spend very little time practicing their craft and improving their relationship skills. Unfortunately, most clients don't care about how smart we are or what we know—until they know we care about them.

The following paragraph is a representation of how one attorney in a meeting presented his solution to my client. He was explaining a buy-sell agreement to this successful entrepreneur who was so conceptual that he rounded off phone numbers. The attorney paid no attention to my client's personality and level of understanding. Here is what this attorney presented to my client; good luck in your own interpretation.

> **Purchase price upon death of shareholder.** For the purposes of this Agreement, the value of the Company's shares shall be an amount equal to two times the excess of the aggregate of its net profits, after taxes, for the five completed fiscal years next preceding the death of the Shareholder whose shares are to be purchased over the aggregate of its net losses incurred during such period. In no event, however, shall the value be an amount greater than 200 percent, nor less than 50 percent, of the book value of the shares as of the date of the Shareholder's death. The value of each share shall equal the value computed in accordance with the above provisions divided by the number of outstanding shares. The net profit or net loss for any fiscal year of the Company shall be the net income or net loss as disclosed on its federal income tax return for that year, except that the capital gains or losses shall be computed at 100 percent, no adjustment shall be made for loss carrybacks or carryovers, and no account shall be taken of any changes in income or loss made by an amended return, by

the Internal Revenue Service, or by the courts. In determining the book value of the shares, the books of the Company shall be controlling. For this purpose, the last regular audit of the books prepared by the Company's accountant shall be accepted as correct, and shall be adjusted by the accountant for the operations from the date of the audit to the date of the Shareholder's death. If any dispute shall arise as to the value of the Company's shares, its accountant shall determine the value in accordance with the above provisions. The accountant's certified determination shall be conclusive for all purposes and upon all parties.

As the attorney finished his presentation, he turned to my client and asked, "Does this make sense to you?"

My client immediately responded with the typical "I'll have to think about it." He then turned to me with a bewildered look and shrugged his shoulders.

I suggested to him the following: "Jim, what he has just communicated to you is that you will be establishing a baseline price for your business that is fair and equitable for both partners. What this means to you is that if something happens to you, you won't have to worry that your family will receive the proper value for your business interests. The real benefit to you is that you can have the peace of mind of knowing that your family members can have the cash flow necessary to maintain their lifestyle. How does that sound to you?"

The moral of the story is, Jim agreed to proceed with executing his buy-sell agreement after I connected the facts through his filter. Complexity, or demonstrating your considerable mastery of facts and minutia, is not what your clients want from you. Leave that kind of talk to the experts to discuss among themselves. Your competence, of course, is essential, but your role is to connect rather than confuse clients by distilling complex problems into simple solutions.

To build out your information and deliver it in a more effective manner, utilize the bridges presented to you in Chapter 6 on building your Personal Value Statement. These are, once again:

- State your fact.
- What this means . . .
- The benefit is . . .

By utilizing this format you will connect with both left brain and right brain thought processes. The left side will analyze the information, and the right side puts it all together. Without communicating in this manner, your information has at best a fifty-fifty shot of being communicated effectively.

Take the time to list all of the key facts, features, and product elements that you normally discuss with prospects and clients. Create this list and then develop your *value statement* for all this information. As you communicate with your clients, insert these statements into your presentation. Experience it for yourself and observe the difference in your meetings. To the extent that you communicate these points clearly and effectively, you will be able to better align what you say with what you mean.

FROM COMPLEXITY TO SIMPLICITY

The longer I am in practice, the more attention I pay to reducing complex subject matter to simple and understandable terms. I share this story with you as an example of how the Trust Factor Question combined with the CORE discussion helped this prospect take action and become my client.

Several years ago, an attorney called me to see if I could help him execute the estate plan he had prepared for one of his clients. He shared with me that he had been trying to get the client to implement this plan for over two years. He was extremely frustrated with his client, a contractor who owned a very successful business. He indicated to me on the phone that they were at an impasse.

This lawyer knew about my planning process and had completed documents for several of my clients. We agreed to a meeting with the client, his CPA, and both of us in my office.

The day arrived and in walked big Ed, a rough, burly man wearing jeans, flannel shirt, and muddy boots. Alongside of him were the attorney and CPA, both in stark contrast to Ed in their three-piece suits. I invited them to sit down at a round table, and the meeting began with the attorney making brief introductions and immediately starting to download the specifics of certain revenue rulings and tax codes using technical terms, acronyms, and jargon. Within five minutes, big Ed sat there with his arms crossed, facing away from them and peering out the window. As I was observing all this and listening to the attorney and CPA discuss Ed's estate tax implications, I realized this meeting wasn't going anywhere.

I finally broke in and said, "Gentlemen, since you asked me to be part of this meeting, may I take a few moments and get Ed's answer to one quick question? Would that be okay with all of you?"

They all nodded their permission. I then said, "Ed, what is it that you care about that needs your attention at this time in your life?"

He turned his chair towards me, unfolded his arms, and responded, "I just want to take care of my family business. It's our cash cow and I want to protect it."

I asked, "What is your biggest challenge with accomplishing this objective?"

He replied, "Understanding my options. This stuff is very confusing. I have been spending a long time trying to understand how I could do this." This reminded me why his attorney brought him to me.

I then asked, "What is the opportunity you are looking to capture, and what gets you excited about taking care of your business?"

He responded, "I see it as the opportunity to set up my kids and grandchildren for life financially."

I then asked him, "Who are the most important people that need to be aligned with you to make this happen?"

He responded, "My wife and my children; I need consensus from them. Some work in the business and some do not." He then pointed to the three of us and said, "And I know I need some outside help with this, too."

"Ed," I continued, "what is your experience with planning for your business? Why do you feel so compelled to do this, and why is this important to you?"

His expression changed dramatically and took on a solemn look. "My best friend died two years ago, and I watched his business become obliterated with taxes. I saw how his family was torn apart over this, and how nobody talks to each other. It was a disaster."

I let his comments sink in for a few moments before I said, "Ed, let me see if I can serve you today by explaining this plan another way, would that be okay with you?" He simply nodded. People who know me, know I have a decanter in my office filled with all kinds of candy. I removed a Tootsie Pop from the dish, unwrapped it, and held it out to him. "Ed," I asked, "what is the difference between this Tootsie Pop and a regular sucker?" He looked a little surprised but then answered, "The Tootsie Pop has a chocolate center."

I said, "Exactly. If the Tootsie Pop itself represented your entire estate, including your real estate and your business, and the center represented the liquidity of your estate, which is generated from your business, what would we have to do to the Tootsie Pop in order to get to the liquid cash of your estate to pay taxes in the event of your death?"

He replied, "You have to break the shell."

I then proceeded, "In essence, breaking the outer shell or selling off other assets, such as your real estate, would still not be adequate for paying your taxes. What we are proposing here is to transfer some of the cash from the business, or from the center of the Tootsie Pop, outside of your estate into what is called a "Wealth Replacement Trust." The benefit to you is that on your death, your children will have enough liquidity in that trust to pay your estate taxes, and maintain the business and your real estate, without having to break the outer shell of the Tootsie Pop."

When I finished, Ed took a few seconds and then said, "For God's sake, I finally understand this stuff. After two years and $50,000, it all came down to a Tootsie Pop." He authorized everyone to execute the plan on the spot. The attorney left with his marching orders to complete the documents, the CPA to do all the valuation and cash flow requirements, and I to proceed with obtaining the insurance.

Here is the real gem of the story: Before Ed left, he took the Tootsie Pop off my desk, put the wrapper back on it, and placed it in his shirt pocket. Why do you suppose he did that? He went home and used that very same explanation to his wife and children to explain his estate plan. Our relationship continues today, and we still talk every year about the famous Tootsie Pop estate plan. When he comes in for his annual review, I place one on the table to remind him of the significance of what he has done.

Not all professionals will relate to this story, especially if they view themselves as extremely structured and analytical. However, I can assure you, the other two advisors at that meeting were very pleased with the results we obtained, and reducing a complex problem to a simple solution helped create a win-win scenario for everyone concerned.

Remember, everyone is doing the best they can with what they know. Treating people with compassion and communicating in terms that *they* understand will significantly enhance your value to your clients and to other strategic relationships.

A*uthentic* **T***ruths*

- If you cannot say what you mean, you will never mean what you say.

- People will hear and incorporate only what they understand.

- Everyone is doing the best they can with what they know.

CONTRIBUTE TO CORE

EXERCISE

Think of two priority issues and determine how your product or service can address them using bridge language of the Value Statement.

The Issue: _____

_____

_____

Because . . . _____

_____

_____

What this means is . . . _____

_____

_____

The benefit to you is . . . _____

_____

_____

The Issue: _____

_____

_____

Because . . . _____

_____

_____

What this means is . . . _____

_____

_____

The benefit to you is . . . _____

_____

_____

12

CONNECTING TO YOUR CLIENT'S REAL NEEDS

"The people who get on in this world are the people who get up and look for the circumstances they want, and, if they can't find them, make them."

GEORGE BERNARD SHAW

"The man who really wants to do something finds a way; the other man finds an excuse."

E. C. MCKENZIE

BUILDING TO AN AUTHENTIC MINDSET

Be **clear** intentions are the fuel that drives behavior.

Be **confident** in converting tasks to intentions.

Be **capable** of connecting to your clients' real needs (intentions) by going through their felt needs (tasks).

When I was a young boy growing up, my sister and I would look forward every January to watching the movie *The Wizard of Oz* on TV. It was always shown on a Sunday in the early evening, and we would make it an event. We would put on our pajamas, make some popcorn, and get ready to be entertained. My favorite scene in the movie was the cowardly lion and company entering the forest on the way to the Emerald Castle. The lion sees the sign and approaches it. He then reads the sign very slowly, "I—would—turn—back—if—I—were—you." I would just crack up laughing when he did that. Little did I know that 20 years later I would be in a profession where my greatest challenge was to understand why we all have these "cowardly instincts" in our lives.

You have undoubtedly experienced this for yourself, both personally and professionally. I am sure you do not go to work to fail, and you started your career with the best of intentions. What is it, then, that causes the great disparity between what we intend to do and what we actually accomplish. Napoleon Hill, in his great book, *Think and Grow Rich,* wrote: "The secret is we become what we think about." The question then becomes, What are we thinking that our best thinking got us to where we are today?

In our professional life, we often become frustrated with clients who do not follow through on their commitments. You may connect with them personally, but when this scenario happens, it is because you did not connect with what they deeply care about. Their "I would turn back if I were you" instinct is keeping them from moving forward.

DELAY IS THE WORST FORM OF DENIAL

In an attempt to better understand why people act the way they do and do not follow through, I began by looking at my own life. I observed those times when my will and discipline faded with things like my exercise program. Being Italian-American and loving good food, I noticed that my philosophy of working out was for the purpose of allowing me to eat whatever I chose to, and not necessarily to develop healthy eating habits.

On the other hand, I observed those times in my life when I was totally committed and stayed the course no matter what. I paid particular attention to those times when all kinds of obstacles entered into the scenario yet could not distract me from my desired result. The bottom line was that at those times in my life, I was acting on truth and purpose and recognized I empowered myself because of the meaning I gave to something. The meaning, or purpose, was stronger than the desire to avoid the necessary tasks. I concluded that when I was in this mindset, my intentions were authentic and helped me form a compelling reason to act.

Our ego mind is designed to solve problems, to expect danger, and to brace us for trouble. It signals our survival instinct, and it likes us to stay with things that are familiar to us. It does not like change or risk taking, and oftentimes magnifies our fears when we attempt to change the status quo. The ego does all this, even if the status quo is something we long to leave behind.

TROUBLE AT THE BORDER

The reason most people do not complete what they set out to do is because they focus on what they do not want, rather than what they *do* want. Observe this for yourself by asking someone, "What do you really want to accomplish?" So often the response is, "I'm not sure, but I can tell you what I don't want." They are focusing more of their thoughts and energy on the negative versus the positive. In a practical sense, what they do not want is to do the necessary tasks that go along with a goal or intention they may have. Let's be truthful, no one really likes to do tasks. Think of the tasks in your profession and how you feel about them. Do you enjoy the paperwork, record keeping, etc.? These tasks are the unpleasant necessities that are associated with maintaining your practice. They are not goals that you set, nor are they the intentions you have for your business. When your focus is on the necessary tasks, or the things you do not like to do, you remain stuck at the border without a passport of intentions to help you cross over. I observe this phenomenon all the time in the financial services industry. You know what is required to be "success-ful." Your three primary functions that earn you money are:

1. Be on the phone and make appointments.
2. Attend client meetings.
3. Prospect and promote yourself.

Al Granum, who created "The Art and Science of Building a Life Insurance Clientele," developed a scientific formula that, if followed, will guarantee your success. The problem is, most people do not. The fact is that the industry is suffering from the lowest retention it has ever had at a time when there is more need for quality advisors and more wealth in this country than ever before. The reason that most people do not adhere to the above-mentioned activities is because they are tasks that no one likes to do. Being active in the career does not necessarily mean you are productive. I personally was not motivated with the task of seeing four people per day or being on the telephone until I paid attention to why I would show up at work.

In his great talk, "The Common Denominator of Success," Albert Gray suggested that "successful people do what unsuccessful people do not like to do." He noted that successful people develop the habit of focusing on a pleasurable result rather than the means or tasks required to achieve it.

HIERARCHY OF INTENTIONS, GOALS, AND TASKS

Let's examine the statement "successful people do what unsuccessful people do not like to do." The tasks of your career are the *how* to do something not the why or the *dominant emotional reason*. The tasks are the necessary steps you take to accomplish a goal, but they are not the goal itself. For example, if your goal is to earn $200,000 of income, you will have to perform the necessary tasks of phoning and meetings to complete the goal. Your intention is your direction or aim of your practice, which drives your goals and propels you through the necessary tasks.

Think of your intentions as the fuel or gas in your car. The goal is getting from Chicago to New York. The task is that you must drive the car 875 miles. You may know *how* to drive, and *where* you would like to go, but if you do not have fuel in the car, you are not going to get very far. Intention is the fuel that will drive your behavior.

You may now start to see the correlation between the authentic mindset of behavior, or Be-Do-Have, versus the selling mindset of Have-Do-Be. Top performers are clear about their intentions first, such as to *be* a financially successful entrepreneur, and then they set smart goals and *do* the tasks to *have* a result, such as financial independence in their life.

My intention is for you to internalize this very important understanding. You may have ambition, but ambition without knowledge is like a ship on dry land. Pay attention to the quality of your intentions, for they are the fuel that drives your behavior. Your goals should be something that would make you feel happy if you accomplished them. Your tasks are the necessary steps that when you have finished, you feel relieved. Your feelings about your goals and tasks are how you can easily distinguish the difference between the two. Your intentions set your internal conviction; your goals and tasks are the external effort necessary to produce your desired results.

USING INTENTIONS TO CONNECT

With this newfound understanding, can you now see why your prospects and clients do not follow through on your proposed solutions? In most cases, your solutions are task based, such as:

- Buying insurance
- Creating a will or trust

- Hiring a money manager
- Reducing debt
- Preparing a tax return

These are all tasks that people do not enjoy and simply do not like to do. Therefore, they avoid the action and typically respond, "I want to think about it." An example of this is an attorney who was sharing his estate planning process with me. He indicated that he had sent out an extensive fact-finding profile to his clients *before* he had met with them. He felt this would allow him to be better prepared and, more important, to test the level of the client commitment. I asked him how many of these he received back on a regular basis. He indicated that 20 percent were returned. He seemed disappointed that everyone would not just jump at the opportunity to complete his 50-page profile and return it immediately. I reminded him that he was asking people to do a very unpleasant task *before* they connected with their intention, or why they would go through this process. He may have been clear on his intentions and desired result; however, his prospects were not.

This is why, on meeting with clients initially, you obtain the *dominant emotional reason* that will cause them to take action. As you recall, you obtain this valuable information through the use of the Trust Factor Question. I will repeat it here for your review: *What is it that you care about, that if I can help you focus on and accomplish in the next 12 months, would make you feel happy with your progress, personally and professionally?*

Although you obtain the dominant emotional reason from clients, the question itself does not frame their intention. Clients most likely are not going to be thinking in terms of intentions, goals, and tasks. In many cases, they simply respond with tasks, such as "I have to get started on my estate planning" or "I need to begin to develop a retirement plan for myself" or "I would like to begin an educational program for my children." Your role in the meeting is to simply observe the answer and pay attention to the meaning behind it. For example, if the client shares with you they

GOAL CONVERTER	
Goal	**Intention**
Buy a house	To be financially successful
Run a marathon	To be physically fit
Move into a new office	To be a successful entrepreneur
Take kids to Disney World	To be a good parent
Create a savings plan	To be financially sound

Sample Intentions:

To be a successful entrepreneur
To be an industry transformer
To be a good provider
To be a person of impact
To be a humanitarian

Sample Goals:

Earn $100K
Increase your client retention
Buy a house
Run a marathon
Mentor a peer

Sample Tasks:

Create a will
Buy insurance
File a tax return
Take a physical
Balance your budget

want to set up an educational program for their children, give them feedback something like this: "If I am hearing you correctly, it sounds like your intention is to be a good provider to your children, is that correct?" Have the courage to do this, for it is vitally important to making the connection. If you do not state it correctly, your prospect or client will most likely state it for you. The key is to engage the answer and give the prospect the opportunity to *be* something first.

If your prospects or clients connect with being good providers, then I would take them through the CORE discussion and focus on the challenges, opportunities, relationships, and experiences associated with being a good provider. In those rare occasions where a prospect may not choose to answer the Trust Factor Question or engage you for a CORE discussion, make a business decision and choose to walk away. If they are not clear on their intentions and not willing to set goals and do the necessary tasks, you are both wasting your time.

CONVERTING TASKS TO INTENTIONS

Once you have a clear understanding of this *intentions-goals-tasks model*, you will provide a whole new level of understanding to your prospects and clients. Many of them do not have this understanding, and as you share it, you will see the lightbulb going off in their head. No one else will have taken the time to help them distinguish the difference between their intentions, goals, and tasks, and why they may be stuck in neutral.

Joe D., financial representative, took this concept and dramatically changed the direction of his practice and the impact he has on his clients. He shared an experience with me of how he engaged a client and asked the Trust Factor Question. The first thing the client responded favorably to was Joe's conversational tone versus a sales presentation approach. Joe then went on to share that the client, worth $5 million, wanted to focus on the direction of his life not his money. Joe took him through the CORE conversation, and they identified all the concerns that could be eliminated and opportunities that the client was excited about. The result of the meeting was that the client shared with Joe he had not focused on his life issues in a very long time and really enjoyed the meeting. The client came to a new understanding that his real intention was to be a better father and husband first and then do things with his money that would demonstrate that. The result for Joe was a sizable commission, and more important, a significant client relationship.

Another example the sports-minded will connect with is the coaching ability of Phil Jackson. He is renowned for his ability to relate to different personalities and make the necessary adjustments to find a way to win.

Let's look at his model and see how it applies. At every training camp, his intention is to win the NBA Championship. He then sets team goals as to how many games they must win in order to achieve that result. The tasks necessary are to prepare the practice schedule, skills development, relationship management, and, most important, *the game plan*. As each game progresses, he will recognize that his game plan is working or not working. If the opposing team presents a new obstacle, such as a different defense, he will make the critical adjustment necessary to *change his plan*. He will also change players in various roles to counter the defense. The result has been nine NBA Championships and the highest winning percentage of any active coach in the NBA.

Note the following: Phil Jackson did not change his intention to win the NBA title, nor did he change his goal of winning a certain number of games. What he had to change was the *plan or tasks* necessary in reaching his objective. Your prospects and clients face this same scenario with their game plan of life. By helping them state an intention and develop smart goals, you let them know in advance they will have to make game plan changes on a regular basis. Remind them of the fact that buying insurance or developing an asset allocation model and creating wills and trusts are tasks. Bring them back to why they would do these tasks in the first place and connect them to their *real need* of feeling appreciated and important. You accomplish this by helping them get through their felt need of comfort by helping them with their goals and tasks.

Let me share with you how this worked in my own life with the decision to write this book. My intention is, *be a leading resource of professional development for the financial services industry.* One of my goals to do this was to write a book. I assure you, the tasks of writing a book are overwhelming. There have been numerous times along the way that the tasks became a challenge to complete. I had to find a publisher, select an editor, do the research, and take the time to write. If I did not consistently come back to my original intent, it would have been very easy to walk away from the project and justify it with what appeared to be logical reasons to do so. The power of my intention drove my internal conviction to produce the necessary effort.

TRANSFORMING INTENTIONS

I have developed this tool that has successfully helped me convert goals and tasks to intentions. I have provided a template of this tool at the end of this chapter. I have also included an Intention Transformer that I completed on myself for your review. Your use of the Intention Transformer will help you connect with your clients' real needs. Your great opportunity is to have them convert those tasks they see as obligations to powerful intentions they view as opportunities in their lives. Help your clients get to their real need of feeling appreciated and important by getting through their felt need of being comfortable with their goals and tasks. What this means to you is to help you connect your clients to their true intentions. The real benefit is that this skill will connect them to you.

Allow me to share with you a compelling story about the use of transforming intentions. My administrative assistant, Naomi Cassier, was part of my team for 16 years. She was the most loyal, dedicated, and trustworthy person I have ever known. Naomi developed breast cancer and was battling it for several years. She took time off for chemotherapy but decided to return to work, despite the fact that she knew she had a tremendous battle in front of her. After another year, her cancer returned and the prognosis was not good. I could see she was in deep pain and anguish over the doctor's latest findings.

I asked her to come into my office to talk about her life. I encouraged her to take some time off, take a drive, and talk with her husband. I asked her to simply focus on one thing, to decide who she wanted to be for the rest of the days that she had left. She initially responded that she did not want to leave me in a lurch with all the projects we had going at that time. I assured her there was nothing more important than her health and what she wanted.

She returned to the office three days later and informed me that she gave a lot of thought to what I had said. She shared with me that for the remaining days she had left, she wanted to *be* a great wife, mother, and grandmother. I congratulated her and responded, "Then that is what you shall be." I encouraged her to do the things that a great wife, mother, and grandmother would do, so she could have the peace of mind of knowing she had spent her last days with the people that mattered most to her.

Naomi passed away two years ago. I, too, am at peace with knowing that I helped her connect to what she deeply cared about in the last days of her life.

A *u t h e n t i c* T *r u t h s*

- We become what we think about.

- Intention is the fuel that drives behavior.

- Our felt need is to be comfortable; our real need is to be content with who we are.

Name _____ The Intention Transformer™ Date _____

INTENTION:
_____
_____

CHALLENGES:
1. _____
2. _____
3. _____

OPPORTUNITIES:
1. _____
2. _____
3. _____

GOALS:
1. _____
2. _____
3. _____

TASKS:

GOAL 1	WHO	DATE	✔
A.			
B.			
C.			
GOAL 2			
A.			
B.			
C.			
GOAL 3			
A.			
B.			
C.			

RESULT:
_____
_____

Name _____ The Intention Transformer™ Date _____

INTENTION:

Be a financially successfully professional in my field.

_____

CHALLENGES:

1. *Work-life balance.*

2. *Conflicting communication dynamics.*

3. *Not using my strengths and talents on a regular basis.*

OPPORTUNITIES:

1. *More wealthy prospects than ever before.*

2. *People are seeking out quality advisors.*

3. *People are unable to do it themselves.*

GOALS:

1. *Obtain 50 new clients.*

2. *Qualify for Top of the Table.*

3. *Earn $500K after business expenses.*

TASKS:

GOAL 1	WHO	DATE	✔
A. *Identify markets*	*Assistant*	*11/1*	
B. *Grade my clients*	*LJC*	*11/20*	
C. *Market survey*	*Assistant*	*11/15*	
GOAL 2			
A. *One hour per day self study*	*LJC*	*10/20*	
B. *Schedule 3 per day*	*Assistant*	*11/1*	
C. *Submit $25K premium per week*	*Team*	*10/31*	
GOAL 3			
A. *Hire quality CPA*	*LJC*	*11/1*	
B. *Create incentive plan for team*	*LJC*	*11/1*	
C. *Quarterly review of goals*	*Team*	*11/1*	

RESULT:

Have financial independence in my personal and professional life.

_____

TAKING AUTHENTIC ACTION

EXERCISE

What will you continue to do? (What is working?) _____

_____

_____

_____

What will you stop doing? (What is not working?) _____

_____

_____

_____

WHAT WILL YOU START DOING?

State one new intention_____

_____

_____

_____

_____

Engage one new action_____

_____

_____

_____

_____

Envision the result _____

_____

_____

_____

_____

THE COMMITMENT PRINCIPLE

Honoring Your Agreements

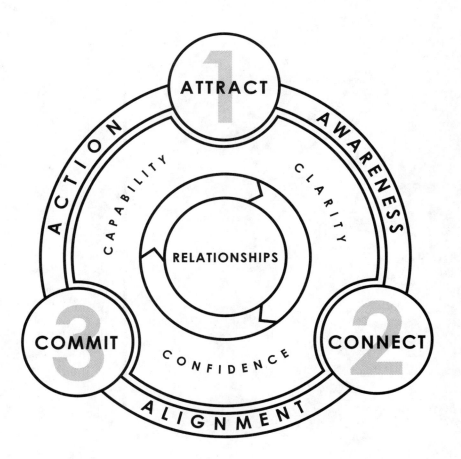

13

THE MOMENT OF TRUTH

*"Nothing is more difficult, and therefore more precious,
than to be able to decide."*
NAPOLEON

"We cannot become what we need to be by remaining what we are."
MAX DE PREE

We live in a time that is considered a golden age. We in America are extremely fortunate to live in the richest land that ever existed, a land of abundant opportunity for everyone. Those of us in the financial services industry recognize that there is more wealth than ever before in this country—and more need for our products and services.

The question before all of us is, "Why do we take all this for granted?" Why is it that only a select few, or 5 out of every 100 people, effectively get to the age of 65 and are able to call themselves successful. There continues to be such a large disparity in what people intend to do and what they actually accomplish.

In this section, we will focus on the essence of commitment. It is very simple to understand, but much more difficult to accomplish. The essence of commitment is simply that *to get a commitment, you must make a commitment.* I observe that far too many people have the attitude of entitlement versus opportunity. They want people to do things for them without necessarily adding value in their work or relationships. Essentially, the majority of people has no clue why they get up in the morning, what they can do, or how they can serve others. They are stuck in the Have-Do-Be mentality and cannot see the forest for the trees.

To effectively build to an authentic mindset, you must be willing to take the position that you will make the first commitment to others before expecting them to make one in return. In your personal life, in order to have a friend, you must be a friend first. You must have an attitude of "willing" versus "wanting" in your life. Being willing is simply the power to say "yes" even in the midst of doubts, worries, fears, and dislikes. Being willing is your ticket to a life of creativity, power, and fulfillment. It will change the course of your life. I am sure there is not a woman in the world who *wants* to go through the discomfort of childbirth, but she is willing.

Being willing is your ticket of admission to your potential greatness. Let me share a story of a young man who was willing to change his life. I first met Brian while making a speech in Orlando, entitled "Experience Your True Potential." He drove up from Naples, Florida, where he lived and worked as a trainer, coach, and client services representative at the Ritz-Carlton. We briefly exchanged pleasantries before my talk, and Brian seated himself in the first row. For the next two hours, I noticed he never broke eye contact and was totally absorbed in my message. After my talk, I always mill around with the audience to connect with them. Brian once again surfaced and shared his vision of who he was and what he wanted to do with his life. On my return to Chicago, I decided that I needed additional staff for The Cassara Clinic and my workshops. I thought of Brian immediately and contacted him to see if he would be interested in working with us, even though I was not specifically sure what the job description would entail. He then informed me he had just taken a new position with Home Depot and was unable to accept my offer. I wished him good luck and called the next person on my list, who immediately accepted the opportunity.

Several hours later, I received a phone call from my assistant indicating that Brian had called all excited. He had refused the position with Home Depot and was coming to Chicago. In the interim, we had hired someone else, so she asked me, "What would you like me to tell him?"

Without even hesitating, I told her that if he was *willing* to come to Chicago, leaving his family and friends without any expectations of what his duties were or what his income would be, she should call him back immediately and welcome him to our team. It is interesting to note that the other people interviewing for the position were more concerned about the benefits I offered them than in how they could benefit the company.

The point I am emphasizing with this story is that Brian was *willing* to make a change in his life and a commitment to someone before he received one back. He initially questioned if he was ready and had the appropriate skill sets. He had to deal with the hassle of physically moving himself from one state to another. He knew very little about the dynamics of my business. There would have been many good reasons why he could have chosen not to take the chance. Some people have to move to another state to change their life. Others just have to change their state of mind.

Brian's dominant emotional reason in his life is to impact people's lives and help them live a life that works. He has made a great impact with The Cassara Clinic and coaches our clients with tremendous dedication and compassion. The result of his courage and commitment is that he has built a thriving practice and consistently expresses an attitude of gratitude to me and everyone he comes in contact with.

GO WITHIN OR GO WITHOUT

As I shared earlier, most people are anxious to improve their circumstances but unwilling to improve themselves. They get caught up in the force of conformity, which basically reinforces the message that to go along with the crowd is rewarded and failure to conform is punished. We are consistently bombarded with messages that suggest we are not good enough. People are constantly telling us what is or is not possible, what we are or are not capable of. We create our own methods of self-sabotage and truly demonstrate what Marianne Williamson observed: "Our greatest fear is not that we are inadequate, our greatest fear is that we can be more powerful beyond measure."

We all pay a great price for this conforming and inauthentic life. It is evident everywhere we look. We cannot even watch a TV show these days without seeing advertisements for antidepressants. The number-one legal drug in this country is painkillers. We are spending billions of dollars per year masking our pain, disappointments, frustrations, fears, and dissatisfaction. At this time, *how* we think is more important than *what* we think. The *what* we think is handed to us and does not appear to be working. *How* we think comes from inside of us. Now is the time for thinking people to think.

Why am I telling you this? All progress begins by telling the truth. There are a lot of so-called leaders out there who are ranting and raving, talking about change, who never go there. There are a lot of tough-guy, macho businessmen creating large injustices in the workplace in the name of business. They use a slash-and-burn style of leadership with employees and clients, and they wonder why they cannot create and sustain significant relationships. Profits may be up in these companies, but spirits are down.

The *moment of truth* before you is to achieve clarity of what has to be done in your life personally and professionally. It is time for you to stop talking so much about the quality of your products, services, and financial statements and start talking more about the quality of your relationships, communication, and promises made to each other.

BEING WILLING COMES FIRST

In order for you to make an effective quantum leap in your business, you will have to be willing to make certain adjustments. If you want to know if something is true for you, ask yourself how you feel about it. Ask yourself the following questions: *"If the process I am using to engage relationships is to be the process that we all have to follow, would I change anything?"* The second question is, *"If the way I am acting is to be the model for all of us to follow, would I act differently?"* Ask yourself these tough questions, because you will never be able to change any action in your life without first examining your underlying beliefs about something. This is easier said than done, but the results can be significant. There are far too many books on the market that tell you how to *do* something, but very few that tell you how to *be* something. Take the time to work on yourself and your business. *Be* your best client, first, last, and always. Build your success from the inside out.

Remember, *to get a commitment from someone, you must make a commitment to them.* Be clear on articulating who you are, what you do, and how that will serve your prospects and clients. Be confident in your ability to connect by understanding and activating the deep emotions in yourself and other people. Be capable of making a commitment first to yourself, so that the information that follows in this section will be more impacting to you and the people you serve. Pay attention to *why* you will do something. It is the *why* in your life that empowers you, not the *how*.

There is one significant point I want to leave with you here. Pay attention to the fact that everything you have ever done in your life that was worthwhile was accomplished by you going into your discomfort. Remember the college you selected and how you left home for the first time? The new home you purchased with a substantially higher mortgage and how you came out okay? Remember how you felt when you watched your kids leave home for the first time? Pay attention to something very important about how you make decisions. Notice that you had an initial feeling, you acted on a value, and you ultimately made a decision. When you think about this experience, the only time you have ever grown or learned something is when you left your comfort zone and went to a place of discomfort. That is where your lessons are—and where your greatness lies.

This tool will help you to understand your own decision-making process, which in turn will show you how others go through the same process. Remember, never discount how others make decisions. Each of us goes through our own process, even though how the process functions is the same. The choice to take action is first, feeling based; second, value based; and third, result based. In this tool, look at the following four questions and ask yourself how you decided to engage your career.

A *uthentic* **T** *ruths*

- Knowing why you do something empowers you, not how to do it.

- You cannot change an action without first changing its underlying beliefs.

- Our life begins at the end of our comfort zone.

HOW YOU MAKE DECISIONS

EXERCISE

Think of a time when you made a good decision, the situation and the factors you weighed.

What feelings led you to make the decision?

_____
_____
_____
_____
_____

What values guided your intentions and actions?

_____
_____
_____
_____
_____

How did you feel after you made the decision?

_____
_____
_____
_____

What did you learn from your experience?

_____
_____
_____
_____
_____

14

VISION PRECEDES ACTION

"Nothing happens unless first a dream."
CARL SANDBURG

"Take charge of your thoughts, you can do what you want with them."
PLATO

BUILDING TO AN AUTHENTIC MINDSET

Be **clear** you become what you see yourself to be.

Be **confident** you can modify behavior by managing emotions.

Be **capable** of helping your clients SEE what is possible.

Imagine if you will that it is a glorious fall day. The sun is shining, and the air is crisp and clean. You are gazing out the window of your beautiful new home waiting for a limo to pick you up to take you to the airport. You are on your way to your industry meeting, where you will be recognized as one of the best at what you do in the world. As the limo arrives, your spouse and children gather around you to give you a hero's farewell and tell you how much they love you. As you drive away and look back at your beautiful home, you realize that it is there because you made it happen.

As you arrive at the conference, you are treated with the appreciation and respect that you so rightfully deserve. You are important to your company and peers. You know you make a difference in your organization and with the people you serve.

More important, your life is balanced. You have enough income and the values to align what you have gained with the proper meaning in your life. You are a true leader, distinguished for your actions in the service of other people.

What would it mean to you personally and professionally to make this a reality? How would it make you feel? What would you be willing to exchange for this vision of yourself in the way of your time, talent, and resources?

In all great endeavors in our life, a vision has preceded the action. A vision is about greatness. It goes beyond the individual. A grand vision is always about others. A vision of greatness focuses on service, adding value and empowering others. A vision is not a mission statement. A mission statement comes from the head, a vision comes from your heart. A vision is a reality that has not yet come to be.

Be clear about your vision, because you will become what you see yourself to be. Visualizing something is the process of creating a clear, sharp, and emotionally charged mental movie of what you want to happen. It is a form of mental rehearsal of things to come, so you can better handle them when they do. The power of your performance is ignited with the fuel of visualization.

In his book, *Peak Performers,* Dr. Charles Garfield states: "The key to success in all walks of life is picturing or visualizing the exact, precise way you want an event to go." There have been many case studies confirming how visualization has provided remarkable results. One example is a concert pianist and former POW who practiced on an imagined keyboard every day in prison. On his release, he was able to play the piano as well as he ever could. Another POW visualized himself playing a round of golf every day. After his release, he was able to score one of the best rounds of golf he had ever played.

Golfing great Jack Nicklaus demonstrates this concept perfectly. In his book, *Golf My Way,* he writes: "I never hit a shot, even in practice, without having a very sharp, in-focus picture of it in my head. It is like a color movie. First I see the ball where I want it to finish, nice and white and sitting up high on the bright green grass. Then the scene quickly changes and I see the ball going there; its path, trajectory, and shape, even its behavior on landing. Then there is a sort of fade-out, and the next scene shows me making the kind of swing that will turn the previous images into reality. Only at the end of this short, private Hollywood spectacular do I select a club and step up to the ball."

YOU WILL PROVE YOURSELF RIGHT

The essence of your life and work is the vision you have behind it. Envisioning what you want is just as powerful as envisioning what you do not want. Both will create results. Your mind acts as an incredible computer; it does not care what vision you place into it and will always provide the means to manifest it.

Let me provide you with an example of this. Imagine that I have handed you a large, plump, freshly picked lemon. I then ask you to cut it in half and place it in the palm of your hand. Feel the weight of the lemon in your hand and observe the juices oozing out of the lemon, running down the side, and creating moisture in your palm. Now, take this lemon and bring it up to your nose and observe the aroma. Now imagine yourself taking a bite out of this lemon and chewing on it. Ask yourself what is going on in your mouth, and then ask yourself if you really have a lemon in your palm.

This is one of the most powerful and yet overlooked elements in the communication process. If you consistently focus your vision on the negative, you will react as if it were already true. How many times have you observed someone in a game of golf say, "I hope I do not hit the ball in the water," and that is exactly what they do?

When you consciously place your focus on a positive outcome and result, your mind and body will produce that as well. The key is to be clear about what you want, because in the final analysis you will prove yourself right.

IMAGINATION VERSUS WILLPOWER

When imagination and willpower are in conflict, imagination will always win out. This statement can best be illustrated by sharing an experience with you. In 1995, I was diagnosed with avascular necrosis, a diseased hip joint, from playing baseball and football all my life. As a former athlete, I initially took the tough-guy approach and said, "I will beat this thing, work out, take the shots, shark cartilage, or any method to avoid having hip replacement surgery." The disease progressed at such a rapid pace that my wife was concerned I might have something more significant or serious such as bone cancer. I literally was walking like I was crippled, dragging my right leg behind me everywhere I went. People used to tell me that it was painful just to look at me.

My willpower was such that I continued to resist the chronic pain for over two years. I could barely sleep or concentrate, and it really was affecting my performance. I was tired, irritable, and could not concentrate. I continued to read about the subject, take more "miracle cures," and struggle throughout the day.

Two years later, my wife and I were asked to chaperone our daughter's dance team to Florida, where they were to perform in the Citrus Bowl. Part of the experience for the girls was to visit Disney World and spend the day at the park. As chaperones, we were to escort the girls and participate in the day. On entering the park and walking for several hours, I just could not take the pain any more. Every step I took resulted in an electric shock emanating from my hip down through my leg and back. I sat down on the bench and told my wife that I could not go any farther. She replied

"I'm going to get you a wheelchair," and I meekly nodded my head in approval.

She returned with the wheelchair and proceeded to push me around the park for the balance of the day. As I was in the chair, the vision of who I was as a 45-year-old vibrant male suddenly diminished. The thoughts and visions that stirred in my mind, that I could not walk or enjoy the simple things in life, were more painful than the pain itself. I made the decision right there and then that on returning home I would see an orthopedic surgeon and have the surgery. My willpower had run out, and imagining myself as a cripple for the rest of my life was not where I wanted to place my focus. I chose to focus on being healthy and not looking for those brief moments of being without pain.

On the lighter side, the experience did produce one positive result. Being in a wheelchair, the kids enjoyed the fact that we could go through the handicap lines and get into all the venues and rides ahead of the crowd. As for my wife, she was so exhausted from pushing me around all day that I switched places with her for the last hour in the park, and my kids pushed her around. To this day, we all still have a good laugh about that day.

You see examples of how imagination wins out over willpower all the time. Your will and discipline will only last to the extent your vision is behind it. You recognize this in people with addictions. Their will and discipline sustains them to the extent they *see themselves healthy, smoke-free, or sober.*

BY MANAGING AN EMOTION, YOU CAN MODIFY A BEHAVIOR

When you really think about it, the most important role in your relationships with prospects and clients is in helping them manage their emotions. Managing their money is a by-product of first and foremost managing the issues in their lives. You cannot manage their money without talking about the emotions in their lives. It seems so simple, yet we oftentimes forget this simple fact.

To develop a further understanding on this, join me in an exercise that will clearly help illustrate this point.

I want you to imagine a four-inch beam separates you and me by 50 feet. If I asked you to come across this beam while it was placed on the ground, would you have any problem doing so? Your answer would be "probably not." Now I suggest to you that I elevate this beam approximately ten stories in the air and suspend it between two buildings. Would you come across this beam? You may respond, "I have to think about that." What if I say to you that I will give you $1 million to do so? Some of you may say yes, and some may say no. Then I suggest I place this beam 100 stories in the air between two buildings and ask you if you would come across on a windy day with no net underneath. You undoubtedly would say no. If I suggest I will give you $10 million, you still may say no.

Then I suggest to you that your child is on the other side of the beam, and if you do not come across to help, your child may fall.

Before I had even finished this statement, everyone I had asked said without hesitation that they would come across the beam. They would do so even at the risk of their own death to save their child. The point I want to make is that we all have "compelling reasons" in our lives, reasons we would walk the plank or lay down our lives. These situations and events instantly clear the fog, and you know exactly what you would do in that situation. When you can connect with your client in this matter and manage their emotion, you almost always get a predictable result.

Your role as an advisor is to find that compelling reason in your prospects or clients—the reason that will drive their behavior and predict exactly what they will do and say and, more important, the choices they will make.

SEE What Is Possible

The way I accomplish this in client meetings is to first and foremost establish what my clients care about through the use of the Trust Factor Question. Once this information is gleaned and converted to an intention, I simply feed back the response as if the client had already experienced it.

I tap into their imagination by having them SEE what is possible for themselves. I encourage them to "try on their feelings." I remind them that they create this experience with other things in their lives. They try on clothes before they buy them, they test-drive a car, they walk through a house before buying it, etc. The three steps to the SEE process are:

1. **S**tate it (the intentions)
2. **E**ngage it (the action you will take)
3. **E**nvision it (the result or feeling you desire)

State the intention.   In the first step, I ask clients to state their intentions. For example, if the client's intention is to provide a quality education for his children, I might suggest, "John, you indicated that the most important issue for you right now is to concentrate on creating a quality education program for your children, is that correct?" Having clients state their intention is the first form of creating their vision. If for some reason you do not state it correctly, ask them to state their intention in their own words.

Engage the action you will take.   After clients state their intention, I suggest my role in their life is to keep this vision alive and help it become a reality. I remind them that it is my responsibility to meet with them regularly and help them focus on accomplishing this objective within their time period. I will go back to my office and prepare a solution to help them meet this objective. I also remind clients that they tend to spend more time planning a vacation than they do focusing on what they really care about.

Envision the result or feeling you desire.   I then put clients through a visual exercise. I ask them to try on their feelings and imagine this has already occurred. In this example of providing a college education, I ask clients to "imagine it is a beautiful day in June, and you are sitting in the stands watching your child's graduation ceremony. When your child's name is called to receive her diploma, you observe how happy she is as she approaches the podium. You also observe how fulfilled you feel that you were able to honor your agreement to your child to provide her with the opportunity to go to the college of her choice because of the planning you have done. As your child receives her diploma, she looks into the stands to find you and your spouse, mouths the words "thank you," and blows you a kiss. How would this make you feel?" I almost always hear a positive emotion. I then ask, "What would you be willing to exchange in the way of your resources to experience this feeling someday?"

I almost always hear "whatever it takes." You have just found the compelling reason why this person would act, the very thing he or she would walk the plank for in this situation. You have made this client taste the lemon, and once someone gets to this place, he or she almost always acts on it.

I recognize that some of you may say that this is too conceptual for you to do. You may feel that this is outside the realm of your personality, and you may either feel you cannot do it or simply are unwilling to have your client experience this. For those of you who feel this way, let me provide you with another example. You may have meetings with CPAs and attorneys who may be more analytical than conceptual. These people still have a vision; it just needs to be stated a different way. In these situations, you may simply state the vision in a more direct manner:

"Mr. CPA, we both agree that we are here today to do what is in the best interests of our client, is that correct? My role in the process is to provide you with the information necessary, so that you have data you can trust to make the best decision on behalf of your client—to be part of the decision-making process, not opposed to it. I, like you, want the client to feel that every 'i' has been dotted, every 't' has been crossed, and every contingency has been covered, so that he or she can make the best decision based on the information available. Is this aligned with your thinking?"

In this manner, I am still stating a vision that would appeal to someone who was more objective. Remember, vision precedes action. Be clear that you can help people become what they see themselves to be. What this can mean for you is that you can modify clients' behavior by managing their emotions. The benefit is that you will be capable of helping your clients see what is possible and create the desire for them to act.

A u t h e n t i c   T r u t h s

- When imagination and willpower are in conflict, imagination will always win out.

- By managing an emotion, you can modify a behavior.

- You will become what you *SEE* yourself to be.

A VISION FOR YOUR BUSINESS

EXERCISE

SEE what is possible and create a vision for your business.

State it: *(The intention for your business)* _____

_____

_____

_____

_____

_____

_____

Engage it: *(What goals and actions are necessary?)* _____

_____

_____

_____

_____

_____

_____

Envision it: *(The result/feeling you desire)* _____

_____

_____

_____

_____

_____

_____

15

THE FACTORS THAT INFLUENCE DECISIONS

"Watch your thoughts, they become your words.
Watch your words, they become your actions. Watch your actions,
they become your habits. Watch your habits, they become your
character. Watch your character, it becomes your destiny."
ANONYMOUS

"We can do no great things, only small things with great love."
MOTHER TERESA

BUILDING TO AN AUTHENTIC MINDSET

Be **clear** *it is the little things that make a big difference.*

Be **confident** *recognizing the difference between projection and perception.*

Be **capable** *of influencing the outcome of the opportunity.*

An article in the July 21, 2003, issue of *Business Week,* titled "I Love You—But I'm Leaving You," discussed the results of a national poll that revealed a sad but true trend in financial services. An astonishing 66 percent of the executives surveyed indicated they were looking to change their financial advisors. The study revealed that 51 percent were looking to move, because they felt their current advisors were "unethical." Twenty-eight percent indicated they were seeking to make a change due to lack of client service or contact.

The question before us is, How do we feel about this information? Are we concerned or excited about the opportunity? Remember, it is not whether we have relationships, it is what kind of relationships we have. Our clients are on the move. They have experienced the setback in the market in the past three years, and they are basing the way we handle that experience with them as a baseline of the relationship they have with us. The events of September 11 have had a great impact on what people are thinking and feeling. This is not the time to be operating as an unconscious competent.

ARE YOU LIKEABLE?

As part of my professional development, I am always seeking feedback from clients for a better understanding of why they like, believe, and choose to work with certain professionals. Let me share some information with you that was gleaned from the 200 entrepreneurs surveyed on this subject matter.

What clients like about professionals are the following:

- *Showed respect.* They were treated with courtesy and respect regardless of the size of their assets.
- *Paid attention.* They liked professionals who were interested in their opinions and ideas.
- *Communicated effectively.* They liked when professionals spoke on a level that they could understand.
- *Connected through experience.* They liked people who had similar interests and who had an understanding of their industry and type of work.
- *Were fun to be with.* They liked people who they could laugh with and had a sense of humor.

The reasons these clients stated that they disliked professionals and would walk away are:

- *Were pretentious.* They pretended to be something they were not.
- *Answered questions they really did not know the answers to.*
- *Appeared to be an "expert" without being able to back it up.*
- *Were self-centered.* They could not stop talking about themselves and implying their own success. People who talk about themselves, think about themselves.
- *Were manipulative.* They appeared disingenuous and manipulative; translation, clients felt they were being sold.
- *Talked about others behind their back.* This was a big one. They did not appreciate when professionals volunteered confidential information to them about someone else. They had the sense that they would not be able to trust them with their personal and confidential information.
- *Were too serious.* These professionals tended to be too detailed, rigid, and inflexible.

Pay attention to the fact that all of these responses are relationship based and have nothing to do with product knowledge. We keep coming back to the point I made over and over again: *People buy from people because they feel something, not because they think something.*

Here are some of the best ways I know to get yourself fired. The biggest mistakes that any professional can ever make with a prospect or client are:

- *Lie to people.* Failing to tell the truth, stretching the truth, or misrepresenting the truth is the number-one way to create a disconnect from your clients. If you have made a mistake, have the courage to step up and admit it. Your clients can forgive that, but they will never forgive you if they catch you in a lie and you defend it.

- *Hovering over your client.* Pushing your clients to make decisions is an emotional time bomb to them. People are irritated by constant phone calls, insensitivity to their situation, strong-arm tactics, and a this-is-all-about-me attitude. The decision-making process is different for everyone, and you must respect that.

- *Taking your clients for granted.* Some professionals operate on the premise that the longer they have the relationship, the less service they have to provide. The client should just do whatever they say, whenever they say it. Just because clients implemented a previous strategy you suggested to them does not mean that they will simply do this over and over. Instead of using your entire process, you tend to skip steps and just get to the bottom line. You don't keep in touch as regularly or keep clients out of danger. I am sure this was a big bone of contention with many clients in the market adjustment over the past three years.

Pay attention to these likes and dislikes of your prospects and clients. There is a dramatic difference between what you are projecting to them and what they are perceiving about you. Be truthful with yourself and admit where you are wrong and need to make critical adjustments. I personally have learned more from prospects and clients who pushed my buttons and brought these negatives to my attention than from the clients who never said anything.

MAKING A SCIENCE OF YOUR ART

In one of his most popular speeches, "Elephants Don't Bite: Doing the Little Things That Get You Big Results," Joel Weldon asks his audiences the following question: "Have you ever been bitten by an elephant?" Predictably, no one raises a hand. "Have any of you ever been bitten by a mosquito?" Everyone's hand goes up in answer to this question. The point he makes is that it is the little things that get us and potentially can even kill us. In our relationships with our clients, it is the little things we do *first* that show our commitment to them. The perception of your commitment will make or break their decision-making process.

The way you can begin to make a science of your art is by being willing to examine the following areas of your delivery and communication process. By paying attention to these "little things," you can dramatically impact the outcome of the meeting:

- *Preparation.* Your preparation can compensate for a lack of talent. The more prepared you are for your meeting, the more confident you will be. Your physical preparation includes your proposal, visuals, handouts, applications, or anything else that you may need during your meeting. Check the quality of your materials and make sure they project a certain look and feel of quality.
- *Be present and positive.* First and foremost, be mentally prepared for the meeting. Envision the result that you would like to have. Focus on the client and why you are there, what you will do, and how you will serve. Most important, be on time.
- *Personalization.* Personalize, not generalize, your discussion with your prospects and clients. This is a major component to likability and showing your commitment to learn about them *before* meeting with them. Do your homework.
- *Enthusiasm.* Your enthusiasm comes from within yourself. It is caused by knowing your subject matter and believing your prospect or client can benefit from your service. By projecting your enthusiasm and confidence, your client will perceive it and reflect it back to you.
- *Participation.* Do you get your prospects and clients involved in the meeting? Are you making a speech or having a conversation? Do you use probing questions to get an understanding or prompting questions, which may be perceived as an interrogation?

- *Pace.* Do more listening than talking. Do your meetings tend to run slow and boring or quick and stimulating? Remember, your prospects and clients have different levels of understanding and paces at which they learn. Conceptual people like the discussion to be fast paced and keep moving; analytical people like to go slower, be methodical, and focus on the details. Presenting at the right pace to the right prospect can make a big difference.

- *Visuals.* If you use visuals in your meetings, are they an enhancement or a distraction? Far too many times, people hide behind visuals, such as laptop presentations, and do not directly connect with the prospect. If they are used effectively as an enhancement, visuals can double the impact of your meeting. Decide where and when they can be used and use them effectively.

- *Humor.* Humor can be incredibly effective if used in the right situations. Making light of yourself, remembering humorous points about the client, or using humorous news can be a great way to enhance your delivery process. Be mindful that offensive humor, or gender-specific humor, can have a negative impact on your meeting.

- *Handouts.* Do you provide a leave-behind for your prospects and clients, something that is concise and reflects on your key points? Do not leave too much or too little; save something for the next meeting. I prefer to use handouts with bullet points, so that I provide the narrative and the detail. This later serves as a discussion draft or overview of the content covered in our session.

- *Voice.* Remember, in the Mehrabian study, 38 percent of your conversation is based on your vocal inflection. Make yourself understandable and watch the tone of your voice. Try not to be too varied or too monotone. Watch your nonverbal cues as well, such as your body language, your hand actions, and how animated you are. These nonverbal cues represent 55 percent of your presentation style.

- *Words.* Although your words represent only 7 percent of your communication, they can have the largest impact in the outcome of the meeting. The bad words and phrases in the chart on page 157 can shut down the client's mind, create a disconnect, and stall a commitment.

Bad words. Words to avoid using when you are in a sales situation.

Pay attention to the power of these words and phrases, in particular encouraging your clients to *sign* the *contract*. Those two negative words together immediately project to someone that the material is complicated and that they may need their lawyer to review the agreement. By simply saying *endorse* the *paperwork,* you project an entirely different meaning to the action. We have been told from the time we were young adults never to *sign* anything without thoroughly understanding it, but observe how many times you initial something, okay it, or endorse it. These little words have big power with the projection and perceived meaning of two different people.

Sometimes, the most powerful and eloquent words you can ever use with anyone are simply *please* and *thank you.* These little words have so much meaning and impact. They show appreciation and respect for others and project the feeling of reciprocity. Pay attention to the quality and power of your words, as they tend to make all the difference.

FROM SELLING TO SERVING

I know I have said it many times already, but I will say it again: *People dislike being sold but love to be served.* As we discuss the little things that make a big difference, I would like to address the area of attitude in our profession. As you transition from the *selling* to *serving* mindset, from the *me* to *we* approach, I would encourage you to pay attention to your attitude and character. Another way of defining character is *doing the right thing when no one is looking.*

Character: Doing the right thing when no one is looking.

I once heard a cute anecdote about character. A woman who did not pay her taxes on time sends a letter to the IRS and says, "I didn't pay my taxes last year and I have been having trouble sleeping ever since. I am enclosing a check for half of what I owe you. If I continue to have trouble sleeping, I will send you the other half." Indeed, we do have to sleep at night and do the right things when no one else is looking.

Negative behavior patterns make people *go weak,* and powerful patterns *make them strong.* The most powerful patterns of all are love, compassion, and forgiveness. The following represents a shift from negative to positive patterns of behavior that can also make a big difference in your relationships:

- *Forceful to powerful.* Being forceful creates resistance. It is characterized by arrogance and self-serving behavior. Power arises from meaning and truth. It is showcased by humility. Hitler used forceful behavior on people. Gandhi aligned with power and was able to bring the entire British Empire to its knees by standing on a single principle.
- *Hearing to listening.* Hearing is about you, and listening is about your prospect. Listening shows respect, generates ideas, and increases knowledge.
- *Demanding to encouraging.* No one likes to be told what to do. Demanding uses a compliant tone and infers that you *should* do this. Encouraging seeks to guide, not control, and empowers people to take action for themselves.
- *Coercing to leading.* When coercing, you are using limiting, exploiting, and manipulating behavior patterns. When leading, you provide people with information and choices.

- *Demeaning to respectful.* When you demean someone, you steal the meaning of something they think and feel. You discount and belittle it. Being respectful is showing compassion, because prospects and clients are doing the best they can with what they know.

Paying attention to the factors that influence decisions can dramatically increase your awareness of the little things that make such a big difference. In the authentic mindset model, I define a *sale* as "the ability to influence the outcome of the opportunity." With that definition and understanding, consider this: *In every meeting that you have, a sale will be made.* Either you will "sell" your prospect on the reasons why they should work with you, or they will "sell" you on the reasons they will not. *The bottom line is, in every meeting a sale will be made.*

Paying attention to the factors that influence decisions can make a big difference to you. What it can mean for you is the ability to recognize the difference between what you are projecting and what is being perceived. The real benefit is that you will have the capability to influence the outcome of the opportunities presented to you through your relationships.

A u t h e n t i c   T r u t h s

- Clients like professionals who show respect, pay attention, and communicate on their level.

- People buy from people because they feel something, not because they think something.

- In every meeting a *sale* is made, and a lesson is learned.

BAD WORDS

Bad Words (Avoid)	Why	Alternative
Sign	Told to never sign	Endorse, OK, approve
Feature	Fact (boring)	Benefit
Contract	Sounds too legal	Application, paperwork
Suspect	Sounds suspicious	Prospect
Pitch	Unprofessional	Presentation
Deal	Unprofessional	Opportunity
Thank you (at closing)	You benefit	Congratulations
In other words . . .	Suggests person could not understand the first time	To summarize . . .
Let me be honest with you . . .	Suggests that you have been lying all along	To summarize . . .
You know . . .	Is meaningless, sounds bad	To summarize . . .
What I'm trying to say . . .	Suggests that the person is dumb and cannot understand	To summarize . . .

16

EMPOWERING PEOPLE TO COMMIT

"A true commitment is a heartfelt promise to yourself
from which you will not back down."
DAVID MCNALLY

"There is a difference between interest and commitment.
When you are interested in doing something, you do it only
when it is convenient. When you are committed to something,
you accept no excuses, only results."
KEN BLANCHARD

BUILDING TO AN AUTHENTIC MINDSET

Be **clear** that the relationship is beginning, not ending.

Be **confident** to get a commitment, you must make a commitment.

Be **capable** of helping others honor their agreements.

There is a key trend in America today that requires our immediate attention: the decline of trust. An article in the June 3, 2003, issue of the *Chicago Tribune*, entitled "America's Motto: In Few We Trust," cited a survey conducted by the University of Chicago's National Opinion Research Center over a 40-year period. The study revealed that in 1964, 53 percent of Americans agreed that most people can be trusted. In 2002, the results concluded only 35 percent of Americans said people can be trusted.

It is apparent that our actions are not based on thoughtful decisions. People in America today are like corks in a sea of unconsciousness, floating endlessly about and asking the same questions. We are virtually drowning in data but do not have the tools to interpret it. We will only reverse this key trend by consciously paying attention to how we are thinking, communicating, and acting.

As I stated earlier, the essence of the authentic mindset is to operate from the understanding that *all relationships are a reflection of the one you have with yourself.* It is important that you consider your mindset when you engage prospects or clients for their commitment. A simple but compelling adjustment is to rethink whether you are "closing" the prospect or "committing" to them. The word *closing* implies forceful behavior; somebody has to win, and somebody has to lose. A closing environment incites separation, a face-the-enemy mentality where you are defending your position and trying to be right.

In a commitment mindset, you are coming from a place of power. As stated previously, *power arises from meaning.* A commitment mindset fueled with power is associated with compassion and makes people feel positive about themselves. The information presented does not elicit arguments, because it is based on truth. The truth is that health is more important than disease, that life is more important than death, that trust is preferable to cynicism. Being kind and compassionate is preferable to being judgmental and condemning.

Think of individuals who demonstrated great power and how they did so. I would hazard a guess that Gandhi did not have a *closing* meeting with millions of people to align them to his cause. I suspect that Martin Luther King, Jr., did not need a PowerPoint presentation to get people to take action. I am pretty comfortable with the fact that Mother Teresa did not take professional development courses in negotiation or persuasion.

These great leaders all expressed their commitment through humility. The bottom line is, they walked their talk. They encouraged people rather than gave them pep talks. They loved and cared for people rather than limited or exploited them. And probably the greatest quality of all is how they let go of their egos. Ego always was, and always will be, the greatest barrier to leadership.

One of the greatest models to empower people toward commitment in their lives is the Twelve-Step Program created by Alcoholics Anonymous. The business world can learn much from this model, as it has stood the test of time and helped millions of people. The simplicity and power in the program is that it is based on the truth. The preamble of AA is that it renders "no opinion on outside matters." Its 12 steps by which members recover are specified as only "suggestions." The use of coercion of any kind is avoided, and this fact is constantly emphasized and reinforced by slogans such as "one day at a time," "easy does it," "first things first," and, most important, "live and let live."

The essence of AA is that it respects freedom and leaves the power of choice up to the individual. It aligns itself with identifiable power patterns, such as honesty, responsibility, humility, service, and the practice of tolerance, goodwill, and brotherhood. It has no code of right or wrong and avoids moral judgments. More important, AA does not try to control anyone, including its own members.

I have had extensive conversations with my brother, Chuck, who has recovered from a substance abuse problem utilizing the Twelve-Step Program. We have talked at great length about the alignment of the authentic mindset with the principles prescribed by AA. My brother has incorporated *both* into his life, to regain his health and self-respect and his capacity to live a fulfilling life for himself and his family.

WHO YOU ARE SPEAKS VOLUMES

It has been written that "who you are speaks so loudly I can't hear a word you are saying." If you desire to have the ability to empower people to commit to you, you must commit to aligning yourself with powerful attractors. You will attract, connect, and get commitments from people when they view you as courteous and considerate, and you treat them with respect. Professionals who demonstrate these patterns are charismatic winners who are sought out. Show me a professional who operates in a loving, kind, and compassionate way, and I will show you a person who has more clients and friends than they can count.

Look at the people who you make a commitment to in your life. Look at the reasons you stay in relationships and why you leave them. You stay in relationships where you feel appreciated, utilized, enhanced, and rewarded. Your best clients and relationships feel this way about you and treat you accordingly. You do not mind putting in the effort necessary because of the psychic income that comes with a job well done.

In those relationships that you have abandoned, you have done so based on a feeling of being limited, exploited, or manipulated in some way. If you recently changed careers or are considering doing so, it most likely is because of one of these three feelings. People stay in relationships that focus on the relationship. They leave relationships that do not focus on the relationship. It really is that simple.

In essence, what you are looking for in your relationships is the powerful pattern of freedom. You are simply looking to be yourself and will sift through a number of relationships, jobs, and careers in order to find that unique situation where someone simply allows you to be who you are. It is in those unique and special relationships that you are allowed to do your best—and do it to the best of your ability.

A SECRET OF COMMITMENT

The secret of empowering others to commit to you is to honor your own agreements and keep your own promises. A promise is your word, whether spoken or implied, that you shape into physical reality. It is a covenant you make with the world and yourself that says "this shall be done."

Think about this for a moment. When you make a promise you set up an energy imbalance with an expectation. Let us say you call your client and tell him that you will get back to him the next day with a pertinent piece of information. Pay attention to the fact that you create a tension, the expectation of something yet to be done. When you put your word out before you, you create a gap that can only be closed when you do what you say. When the next day comes and you deliver on your promise, you relieve the tension. The energy and the expectation are now balanced.

When we do not honor our agreements and keep our promises, we often neglect to consider the effect. When we do not do what we say, we are left with the tension unresolved. Unfulfilled promises are energy drains, because we tend to spend more energy worrying about them than resolving the issues.

Each unfulfilled promise you make becomes an obstacle to your performance. It saps your power, and you become physically and emotionally tired and lose energy. An important point to consider is, it does not matter with whom you make your promise. Not keeping your word to yourself is still not keeping your word. It is no more excusable than failing to keep your promise with anyone else.

In my humble opinion, the reason there is such a decline in trust in America today is that most people are not honoring their agreements and keeping their promises. The reason they are so quick to recognize truth about someone else is because they know intuitively they are doing the same thing. You cannot recognize a quality, whether good or bad, in someone without being capable of demonstrating it yourself.

You establish trust in your relationships, because you honor your agreements with other people to tell them the truth. As you recall, that is how I defined a great friend: someone who will always tell you the truth. Notice that when your client relationships have become deep friendships, it is because the relationship is based on truthful communication.

DETERMINING READINESS AND COMMITMENT

In the earlier days of my career, I used to think that being aligned with a strong company, and having my own name on the door in a prestigious lobby, could give me power. It took me quite a while to recognize that at best I would have only authority, not power, with my clients and employees. The two are not even close to being the same thing. Authority has more to do with influence, and the real power is with those who have the money or access to money.

Another understanding about being an entrepreneur is the difference between power and control. Power comes only from the people you work with. They give it to you, because they trust you to use it well, and if you do not, they take it away from you. I experienced this many times within my private practice. I would say to my staff, "Okay, guys, I would like you to go out and do this or that in this particular manner."

My beloved staff at times would say, "But Lou, we do not think that will work so well," and I would respond, "I am sure it will work, go for it." In a few days, they came back and shared, "Lou, we tried it the way you said . . . and it did not work."

I was starting to learn some subtle rules of relationships. What I had with my staff was influence and not power or control. Power and control are illusions that we create for ourselves out of our sense of authority. We have this illusion that we control our children, because we are bigger and stronger. Then the truth sets in: Our children control their own lives, and at best, all we can do is influence them.

The same is true with your prospects and clients. The power you have is the willingness and commitment to your clients to carry out your vision. Your clients reciprocate that commitment when they trust you to lead them in the right direction. You never have the power to force them to do the things they do not want to do. You have the illusion of power with your clients, as long as it is used in their behalf. The minute you violate that trust and confidence, they will take it away from you in a New York minute.

This is very apparent by the fact that so many clients are on the move at this time. They have the power, because they have the money, and they are pulling rank on professionals who they feel have not served them in their best interest. This same truth is also evident with management. We give them authority to use on our behalf. To the extent they use it for or against the people they manage will determine how long they keep it.

THE INFLUENCE FACTOR

As a professional, there are always three *sales* that have to be made in order to influence your prospect or client with making a commitment to you. In order to get a commitment, you will need to make sure you have alignment with the client in these three areas. Since I know the client must sign off on all three of these decisions, I am conscious of presenting my information through value statements and testing for alignment along the way. For example, after I present a fact and describe what it means to clients and how they could benefit from it, I then follow up with, "In your opinion, do you feel that this would be an important part of any plan you might consider?"

A "yes" response indicates I have alignment on this point and can utilize it later to build out my final solution. A "no" answer means the client felt it was irrelevant and would not be a necessary component in the final discussion.

I focus on presenting as many value statements as possible during the meeting. I check for alignment with each and every one of them. The more "yes" responses I obtain, the higher the probability of the client committing to working with me.

The most powerful use of the Influence Factor occurs when I combine all the elements together at the end of my process. When I feel I have provided all the information, or have received a buying signal from the prospect, I then ask for the final commitment in this manner: "John, my purpose at this time is to get your answers to a few questions, would that be okay with you?"

I then ask three alignment questions in succession, beginning with the *least* to the *most* important. I initially ask the client for their opinion on these elements and not for a decision:

- ***Product or solution.*** "In your opinion, do you feel comfortable with the product/service/solution I have shared with you?"
- ***Organization.*** "In your opinion, do feel that this company meets your requirements as the fiduciary for your money?"
- ***Yourself.*** "In your opinion, do you feel I have listened to you and developed a solution that aligns with your feelings and values, and that we could have a long-standing client/counselor relationship?"

If prospects or clients say no to any of these, you know they are not ready to make a commitment. Even more important is that you will know why. If your client hesitates on your product or solution, you know the area that needs to be influenced. The same is true for your organization. A *yes* on all three of these alignment questions indicates three green lights for your client to make the commitment to you.

Once you have tested for and feel you have alignment, then ask the client a question that directly asks them for their decision. It is best to always do this by providing a choice, such as "Based on your feelings, would you like to proceed with Plan A or Plan

B?" Provide choices to your clients and never limit them with simply one option. There is another key point in concluding the Influence Factor: *When you ask for the decision about your solution, your organization, and yourself, be quiet. The next person who speaks commits.*

Hopefully, it is your client, at which time you should *congratulate* them rather than *thank* them. Congratulating them will reinforce that *they* benefited from their decision, not you.

My whole process of Client Creation is centered around these three important elements. I know I am ultimately going to ask for the most important decision of all, the decision and commitment to work with *me* personally. By placing my attention on my intention to serve my client and to watch my words, actions, and behavior, I am better prepared and committed to do my very best.

Experience the Influence Factor for yourself. Have the courage to show clients your commitment by asking their decision on you. The benefit to you is that you will be focused and committed to honoring your agreement and keeping your promises with your clients.

Authentic **T**ruths

- Your career is the sum total of the choices that you have made to date.

- Your best relationships are those that allow you to be who you are.

- When you ask for a decision, be quiet. The next person who speaks commits.

THE INFLUENCE FACTOR™

EXERCISE

Devise questions that measure a person's receptiveness to making a decision based on this introduction: "My purpose at this time is to get your answers to a few questions. Would that be OK with you?"

Product/Solution: In your opinion . . .

_____

_____

_____

_____

_____

_____

Company: In your opinion . . .

_____

_____

_____

_____

_____

_____

Yourself: In your opinion . . .

_____

_____

_____

_____

_____

_____

Chapter 17

CONVERTING OBSTACLES TO OPPORTUNITIES

"Success is the ability to go from failure to failure with no loss of enthusiasm."
WINSTON S. CHURCHILL

"Opportunities are seldom labeled."
WILLIAM FEATHER

BUILDING TO AN AUTHENTIC MINDSET

Be **clear** on the meaning of "I want to think about it."

Be **confident** obstacles are part of the decision-making process, not opposed to it.

Be **capable** of allowing others to express concerns openly.

Consider these words written by the author E. B. White: "I arise each morning torn between a desire to improve the world and a desire to enjoy the world. This makes it hard to plan the day."

This statement is so compelling, because it truly identifies and connects with the feeling of so many people. We all face the

191

challenge of finding our real need in life, such as our purpose, by going through our felt need of financial security. Our greatest desire to feel important sometimes is diluted by our need to pay our bills. We intuitively know the difference between doing the right thing and doing things right. The truth is, life requires us to do both.

The most common response you hear from people when you ask them for a commitment is, "I want to think about it." An important factor in converting obstacles to opportunities is to have a thorough understanding of what this answer really implies. So many professionals simply discount the answer and query the client, "How *long* would you like to think about it?" If the client then responds, "Give me two weeks," typically most professionals say, "Okay, I'll give you a call in two weeks then." You then call back in two weeks, only to learn that the client still has to think about it. The real question is, *What are they thinking about?*

To better understand why people almost always respond in this manner, it may serve you to look at why *you* may respond this way. When someone asks you to make a decision or for a commitment, why would *you* say "I want to think about it"?

What you most likely are thinking about is whether you are willing to *stop* doing something in order to *start* doing something. You look at the new challenges and concerns that may be brought about by making this commitment. In an earlier chapter, I described how our ego mind resists change and likes to keep things status quo. In other words, *resisting something is the first step to making a commitment.*

This is a very important understanding that can help you be more compassionate with people in their decision-making process. Some clients will be very quick to decide, and others seem to take forever. The key is in understanding that this resistance is almost always in the form of questions that need to be answered in the client's mind. These questions are normal and necessary and suggest that the client is still interested. More important, if you can answer the questions appropriately, they can lead you directly to what will make the client commit to you. Think of your client's concerns from now on as nothing more than questions in disguise.

In addition to clients asking themselves if they are willing to make the commitment, they will have additional questions about you, your company, or your solution. The use of the Influence Factor, as described in Chapter 16, will help flush out these questions. Clients must have these questions answered in their minds, or they will not commit. A confused mind will always say no.

THE Q&A STRATEGY: RESPONDING TO CONCERNS

Let me remind you here, once again, that you cannot make people do anything they do not want to do. At best, you can influence the outcome of the opportunity by effectively answering the client's questions. *Clients* have the power to write the check, not you. Your role is to facilitate the process of *how* they think about their concern or problem. Here are four steps you can use to respond to your clients' concerns that can help lead them to a decision and a commitment:

1. Respond with reciprocity.
2. Confirm with compassion.
3. Empathize.
4. Empower with emotion.

RESPOND WITH RECIPROCITY

"It appears you have a question, may I ask you what it is?" Keep in mind that questions are the creative acts of intelligence. Give your clients the credit they deserve for having the intelligence to ask you questions. Clients will only transform their experience from *thinking* about something to *acting* on it through their ques-

tions. If they are not asking you questions, the probability is very high that they are not interested.

When you respond with reciprocity, you are demonstrating to your clients that their questions are necessary and normal. Remember the content you deliver to them must go through their contextual understanding of what you said. To the extent you deliver your content clearly and effectively, you will answer many of their questions before they are raised. If not, be prepared to answer their questions in a respectful manner. Do not appear upset or frustrated, as this will create a disconnect.

CONFIRM WITH COMPASSION

"If that question were answered to your satisfaction, would it help you with your decision?" The most important attitude you can convey to your client is a feeling of compassion. People have different levels of understanding and are doing the best they can with what they know. Just because you understand something doesn't mean they do. Their questions are their way of putting your content through their filter to better understand it. By confirming that this question is important, it will guide you directly to what can help them decide.

Clients will answer your question in one of two ways. They can say yes, or they can say no. If they say yes, answer the question and then ask them for a decision. Keep in mind that your clients will pose a question as an excuse simply to stall for time. By saying yes to you, they are thinking about what new challenges their decision creates for them.

Eric K., a financial representative who had gone through our coaching and mentoring process, had seven meetings in a row in which the prospect responded with the normal "I want to think about it." He responded to their concern by saying, "It sounds like you have a question, may I ask you what it is?" The prospect asked his question. Eric then asked if he could answer that question, would it help them with their decision? Each and every time, in those seven consecutive meetings, he answered the question and the prospect took action. Eric was so excited that he called me from every meeting, sounding amazed, to tell me, "Hey, it really works." It seems so simple, but it is very powerful. You are simply confirming what you know, that *it is human nature to resist before we commit.*

Here is another very important understanding. If your prospect says no to *your* question, then they are simply giving you an excuse. An excuse is not a concern. If someone responds no to your question, simply respond once again by saying, "Then there must be another question, may I ask you what that is?" By asking this again, you will flush out the real concern and be able to answer the question. If you attempt to answer an excuse, your meeting will go nowhere. You will find yourself in a crash-and-burn scenario where all you do is irritate the client further by not being able to address the real issue or concern at hand.

EMPATHIZE

"I can understand how you feel. It raises another question, would you benefit from this decision?" In many cases, your prospects and clients may give you a yes answer that needs additional help or clarification. You most likely have experienced this in the form of *maybe.* In these situations, it is important to reassure your clients that they are not Lone Rangers. Let them know that how they feel about their life and money and aligning the two is very normal. Empathize with them by letting them know you understand how they feel. Prospects are really wondering whether they will benefit from working with you and the solution you provide. Be assertive with their "maybe" and address this directly. Convert the soft yes to a definite commitment.

EMPOWER WITH EMOTION

"That could be the very reason . . ." One of the most compelling ways you can help your clients commit is to suggest to them that the reason they are avoiding something may be the very reason they ought to do it. This discussion takes courage; however, it can be one of the most effective conversations you will ever have with your prospects and clients. Help them understand that with every decision they have made, they made from a place of discomfort. Remind them of prior situations in their lives when they felt a similar way, took action, and had positive results. If you are uncomfortable with engaging their concerns head-on, ask for the permission to do so. You may suggest to them, "This may be difficult for me to say, but I feel it is important, may I share my thoughts with you?" Remember, if clients give you their permission, you can ask them anything.

By directly addressing your clients' reasons for delay and appealing to their emotions, it is really in their best interests. You can help them think through the obstacles that are blocking their ability to act and commit. By bringing their reasons to delay out in the open and discussing them directly, you have a chance to convert those obstacles to opportunities for your clients.

There are many ways to respond to your clients' concerns. Keep in mind that you have different personalities to contend with, some conceptual and some analytical. The three categories of responses that I use on a regular basis to answer questions I call SET:

- *Stories.* Stories are a great way to keep people's attention and educate them. Nothing activates others' emotions or enables them to put themselves in a situation to learn more than a powerful story. Convey the points you want to make through the body of the story. Quick anecdotes or analogies can make your point compelling.

- *Evidence.* For people who are more analytical and logical in their process, use facts and empirical data to support your answers. These types of clients will tend to trust your data before they trust you. For example, an engineer, CPA, or attorney will need to "do the math" before committing.
- *Testimonials.* With written permission, give examples of other clients you have worked with who went through similar planning or experiences. Have letters from these clients wherever possible to share. When appropriate, you may have your prospects call a preapproved list of your clients for sharing their experiences with them.

The use of the Q&A Strategy in handling your clients' concerns is designed to guide the discussion, not control or manipulate it. It allows you to handle questions in a very professional manner. More important, it will keep the discussion on track and moving forward. The questions you exchange with your clients will provide you both with the opportunity to share your creative intelligence.

WORTHLESS OR PRICELESS?

Take a moment to think about a scenario that involves one individual and two physicians. Let us say this individual is a male, age 55, overweight, with high blood pressure and generally poor lifestyle habits. He visits Dr. A., who provides him with a superficial exam, reviews his medical history and charts, and suggests to the individual that he watch his diet, exercise, and take better care of himself. The individual pays this doctor $100 for his information and leaves his office.

He then goes to Dr. B., who on reviewing his medical history and charts, asks his patient if he could be truthful with him about his condition. The patient nods and the doctor proceeds to tell him that unless he radically changes his lifestyle habits, his diet, and begins an exercise program, he most likely will be dead in the next five years. He will never have the experience of watching his children get married or enjoy his grandchildren. He further tells him that if he continues on the current path he is on, he most likely will develop late-onset adult diabetes and may potentially go blind and have other related problems. Dr. B. also charges his patient $100 for his time and services. The patient leaves Dr. B.'s office, goes to his pantry, throws out all his junk food, buys a treadmill, and begins the process of changing his lifestyle. The individual paid both doctors the same fee for information, but whose information was worthless and whose priceless?

Think about what you are communicating to your clients in order to help them convert their obstacles to opportunities. Is your information worthless or priceless? *Your information is only priceless to the extent that your clients act on it.* Having a lot of good ideas that never get implemented is like running in place. A lot of your clients are searching for shortcuts around their obstacles and, for the most part, simply do not know how to deal with them.

I am continually reminded of the priceless value of our information whenever I serve my clients through death claims. I have experienced firsthand a spouse thanking me for the vision and planning that invariably protected their lifestyle and possessions. While everyone else is calling to collect money, I am the only one bringing a check to the family. In these special moments, I know what I do is *priceless*.

STRATEGIES FOR COMMITTING

I would like to share with you some strategies for discussion that have been very effective for me in helping people think about their obstacles and take action. I use these strategies to provide people with another way to look at something that may stimulate their thinking.

Vision/Real play. This discussion is centered around allowing the client to "test-drive" a certain experience. My intent is to see if what they say and how they feel are really in alignment. An example would be a wealthy parent who refuses to do planning for fear of spoiling his children. I suggest to him that he will be "remembered for the last thing he does," and I invite him to experience and try on his feelings about his legacy. I describe a scenario where he dies suddenly, and after the service his wife, banker, and business partner call to set up a meeting. I ask him to "real play" with me what these three people might ask me about the planning he has done. I walk him through all the potential questions and ask him how he would feel about the responses I would have to give them. I do not challenge him, or judge his answers, I simply give the prospect the opportunity to experience it. I will usually make light of it as well by indicating most people do not have the opportunity to come back from the grave and ask themselves these questions. When I complete the discussion, I simply ask the prospect, "Do you still feel the same way you did before?" In many circumstances, I have had a complete reversal of attitude and direction, and the client has made a commitment to act.

Cost versus investment. With this discussion, I explain the difference between the cost of something and the price of something. I frame the discussion by asking the prospect, "Why do you own your home rather than rent it?" The prospect proceeds to tell me the reasons—building equity, tax advantages, appreciation, etc. Within this framework for discussion, I then make the analogy that buying a lower-cost product is like renting. It may be an initial savings in "cost" in the short run, but it is actually much more expensive in the long run. You can use the same analogy with leasing or purchasing a car. The renting-versus-owning analogy is effective in helping people connect a known to an unknown. They can also relate to basic investment and tax implications, which can be helpful in converting your more complicated examples.

Instruction/Action. With instruction/action, you can offer your solution one step at a time. You can use this strategy to respond to "no hurry" or "no need at this immediate time." In many cases, people do not commit because they view your process as a hassle, time-consuming, and complicated. I suggest to the client that they could take "baby steps." They can do the process one step at a time. In many cases, the next step may be to simply set the next meeting with other advisors. Break your process down into pieces and eliminate the hassle for your prospects and clients. The easier you could make it for them, the more likely they are to follow through.

Opportunity versus obligation. I use this discussion to present planning as an opportunity to create something, rather than an obligation to simply do something that someone else suggested. I suggest to prospects that they can choose to create an estate with or without my solution. I then outline and share the specific advantages and disadvantages of each way. I explain the best case and worst case scenarios of a proposed solution against the risk of prospects doing nothing at all. If you can show them how your solution is an opportunity to create something and not an obligation to do something, they will place a much greater value on your recommendation—for example, the difference between creating a retirement lifestyle with freedom versus the obligation to pay estate taxes. In many estate planning cases, the cost of doing nothing will far outweigh the cost of the solution. I remind the client that the premium is not the problem, it is the solution to the problem.

Procrastination. I use this discussion when prospects continually delay making a commitment. I explain the emotional and practical downsides of delay. I present the current cost of taking action versus waiting until sometime in the future. Every year they wait, the harder it is for them to catch up to their initial objective. This *cost of waiting* can be considerable in both insurance and investment planning. I also discuss emotional implications, such as the potential risk of losing insurability and not being able to have this planning option available to them in the future. In many scenarios, I simply go over the pros and cons of taking action, and it simply and clearly illustrates the real cost of delay, both emotionally and financially.

The intent of these discussions and strategies is to put clients in a safe environment to express their concerns openly and freely. The only time you should not expect to have concerns or questions is when you are making a speech. Otherwise, expect and welcome questions as the acts of creative intelligence they can be for both of you. Develop your own examples and stories around these strategies to make your main points. Be creative, have fun, and bring a different perspective to your prospects and clients.

One last point on allowing others to express their concern openly and freely: Avoid the tendency to defend your position, and *do not ever challenge a client's belief*. If your prospects or clients feel challenged at any time, you can be confident you will be excused in a hurry. The quickest way to create conflict in the relationship is to act defensive and want to be right at all costs. Challenging your clients' beliefs about something is like attacking their religious convictions. You will never get anyone to commit to you or your ideas with that mindset.

I would like to conclude this chapter by sharing one last strategy for you to experience and internalize for yourself. I call this my self-evaluation discussion, which I oftentimes use with prospects and clients to help test alignment of their intentions, goals, and results they would like to have. It is simply a series of questions that I ask to help them think through how they make decisions. Let me now present it to you for your consideration.

If someone came to you with an idea or opportunity, what would you do? The first question you might ask yourself is the following: "If I were to invest my resources (time, money, energy, and life) in this activity, what is the best thing that can happen?" Second, "What is the worst thing that can happen?" Third, "What is the most likely thing to happen?" If the most likely thing that can happen will move you closer to your goals and intentions, and you can handle the worst that can happen, then decide and commit to do it.

A *u t h e n t i c* T *r u t h s*

- Nineteen out of 20 clients are going to generate at least one question or concern before making a commitment.

- It is human nature to resist before we commit.

- Questions are creative acts of intelligence.

ANSWERING CONCERNS

EXERCISE

Choose a concern posed by your prospects and answer with a Q&A Strategy.™

Objection/Concern:

_____

_____

Respond with reciprocity: "It appears that you have a question. May I ask what it is?"

_____

_____

Confirm with compassion: "If that question was answered to your satisfaction, would that help with your decision?"

_____

_____

Empathize: "I can understand how you feel. It raises another question: Would you benefit from this decision?"

_____

_____

Empower with emotion: Answer the question, "That could be the very reason . . ."

_____

_____

Envision the result: "Try on the feeling . . ."

_____

_____

Ask for the Commitment

ALIGNING STRATEGIES

EXERCISE

Identify three strategies that you align with to utilize in your process.

Strategy One

_____

_____

_____

_____

_____

_____

Strategy Two

_____

_____

_____

_____

_____

Strategy Three

_____

_____

_____

_____

_____

C h a p t e r

18

ALIGNING INTENTIONS
WITH ACTIONS

*"If you want something you have never had,
you will have to do something you have never done."*

LIN TEAGLE

*"Change and growth take place when a person has risked himself
and dares to become involved with his own life."*

HERBERT OTTO

BUILDING TO AN AUTHENTIC MINDSET

Be **clear** *leadership is not what you do, it is what others do because you are there.*

Be **confident** *all progress begins by telling the truth.*

Be **capable** *of impacting the lives of others.*

Have you ever sat around in a quiet moment and asked yourself, "When will my life finally take off?" What does it take to "get it together" and achieve success? Why can't I do what I really want to do with my life and still make a living?

Whether you consider yourself struggling and tired or successful and inspired, the truth is you are where you are today because of who you are. To change your life and get it to take off, you must first change your thinking about it. Your biggest challenge to putting it all together is to be *clear, confident,* and *capable* of being responsible to yourself and in the way you think, speak, and act. You will get your life to take off by first becoming very clear about who you are, what you will do, and how that serves others. You build your authentic mindset by thinking about this vision of yourself and nothing else. When you imagine there is no other possibility but the result you desire, you will then see your world as the result of your thinking about it.

This is easier said than done, and where being willing is so critical to change. Being willing to change is the first step and requires the most energy, just like a rocket taking off. A rocket will use the majority of its fuel on takeoff and later fly with ease through zero gravity. Being willing to change will launch you through the challenge of procrastination and propel you towards your vision. You are the only one with this fuel and power; no one else can supply it but you. If you are unwilling to do something, no one else can lend you the fuel to do something you are not willing to do.

BLIND SPOTS TO YOUR VISION

Helen Keller was once interviewed and asked, "Is there anything worse than being blind?" She responded, "Yes, to be without a vision." Your vision of yourself is critical, because it precedes your actions. However, life does not reward vision, it rewards actions. Here are some of the more common blind spots that keep us from aligning our intentions with our actions.

Failure to recognize opportunity. Most opportunities appear in our lives at what seems to be an inappropriate time. They present themselves in disguise and, in many cases, are not readily obvious to us. We tend to misunderstand them, view them as a distraction, and simply leave them unattended.

Think about a certain time in your life when someone presented an opportunity to you that you viewed as a distraction initially and later wished you would have not ignored. People are presenting these to us all the time, and if we are not clear on where we are going or who goes with us, it will be difficult to *see* the opportunity.

Denial behavior. Not paying attention to our vision can easily take us out of alignment. When we feel we are trading our passion for security and not enjoying our work, we create psychological trade-offs that impact performance. We may show up late to work, leave early, take sick days (and come back with a tan), waste time, or take long lunches.

Delay is the worst form of denial. When we are psychologically out the door, it is usually because we are not utilizing our strengths and abilities in a productive manner. Our talents and strengths are needs, and if not, they become symptoms of our behavior.

The force of conformity. We are easily conditioned as human beings to our surrounding environment. Every human community—church, family, corporation, school—passed along the message that conforming is rewarded and failure to conform is punished. We are bombarded with the message that we are not good enough. These messages imply what is or is not possible for us, or what we are or are not capable of.

We tend to develop a method of self-sabotage around this force. For example, perhaps you have shared your newfound enthusiasm to create a new business with your most cynical family member. You might as well have hit yourself on the hand with a hammer, because you most likely walked away with the same result.

Resisting wake-up calls. When we are out of alignment with who we are and what we do, we are not as willing to turn our receiver on and get the message from people and situations that we could learn from. Some relationships will no longer work, and we may discount certain lifestyle calls and not take care of ourselves physically. Performance calls at work tend to come in the form of strained relationships and a feeling of boredom and frustration.

Confusing activity for productivity. If we truthfully watched how we spend our time, we would notice that we spend approximately 10 percent of our day actually doing things that earn a living and 90 percent creating dramas and circumstances to justify getting up in the morning. You most likely know or have experienced someone who always appears to be "working" late into the evening yet consistently has less productivity than others.

Another way to look at this is to examine a professional football game. Although it may take three and a half hours to complete, there is only between 13 to 15 minutes of actual playing time. The rest of the time is used to create the drama and circumstances around the game and justify the ticket price.

Defending your point of view. Nothing can knock us off-center and out of alignment faster than trying to be right all the time. The question we have to ask ourselves is whether we want to be right or be happy. When we choose to be right, we tend to use force, be restrictive, and hold on to everything. If you have been in the presence of someone who is "always right," you get the impression that they play small and that everything is about them. You may also have experienced two people with conflicting views who turn to you and ask you, "What do you think?" It is a no-win situation for all parties involved. I have a suggestion: If this happens to you, and you perceive an argument may come of it, simply say, "You may be right about that." You will quickly diffuse the tension and confrontation.

When we choose to be happy versus being right all the time, we let go of the negative energy and focus on positive results. To be for something, like serving, versus against something, like selling, puts all our positive energy and thoughts on producing the desired results. A classic example of this is spending time worrying about not doing an activity, such as self-study, instead of investing 30 minutes per day to develop mastery.

Waiting for the perfect moment. Has anyone ever told you that you think too much? Do you tend to resist taking authentic action by studying something to death? There is always one more angle to consider, one more expert to consult, or one more skill to acquire. The result often is a bureaucratic gridlock within your own thought process, causing you to freeze up like an ice cube.

The perfect moment never seems to come, the watched pot never boils. We tend to choose a parallel path to our vision and intention. We stay close enough to keep our eye on it, but not close enough that we are tempted to make the full commitment. It is like a kamikaze pilot who flew 100 missions: He was involved but not committed.

There are many examples of this in everyday life. Someone may choose to be an art critic instead of an artist, a talent agent versus a performer, a teacher versus a parent, or an editor versus a writer. This situation reminds me of a person standing at a crossroads contemplating two signs: the first indicates the way to wealth and happiness, the second to workshops on how to be wealthy and happy.

SEEING THROUGH NEW *IZE*

Dedication to do something expresses itself as commitment. When we decide to make our vision real and experience it as if it were already happening, life reciprocates. It draws people and resources to us. Insights and ideas come to us. We recognize synchronicities in our lives, and opportunities just seem to present themselves to us.

Here is a model that you can use to start seeing yourself through new *IZE*. By making a commitment to yourself, a promise that you will not break, you can align your attentions with actions. Experience the following:

- *Visualize.* State your authentic vision. An authentic vision is always about others. Your greatness lies in what you offer another person. Relationships are the greatest tool to experience who you are. A vision's greatness is about *service,* and it comes from your heart, not from your head.
- *Energize.* Look at your current situation as it relates to your vision. Whatever you place your attention on expands. You may start this process by focusing on your relationships and then moving to your finances and business. The key is to be willing to look at something.
- *Mobilize.* See something for what it is. In this step, it is important to examine what is working and what is not working for you. Pay attention to what you will continue to do, what you will stop doing, and what you should start doing. In this step, you will *see* what is going on in your relationships. Are they superficial and shallow or sustaining and significant? This step requires courage to separate fact from fiction and to simply recognize something for what it is.
- *Internalize.* Tell the truth. You have to be willing to tell the truth about what you see. There is a difference between the truth and being honest. The truth is what is. Being honest includes your thoughts, feelings, judgments, and emotions. For example, the truth is what you earned last year. Being honest about it will reflect how you feel about it.
- *Realize.* Take authentic action. If confusion is the first step towards wisdom, then clarity is the first step towards mastery. Set an authentic intention, that is, an intention that is aligned with your vision. Complete the Intention Transformer exercise, which addresses the challenges, opportunities, important relationships necessary to assist you, and your prior life experience. By assessing this information, you can set goals you are excited about and focus on the

tasks required to complete the goals. The key is to take a *first step,* even if it is a small one.

Let me provide you with an operative example of how this process may work for you. If your authentic vision is to be an *industry leader,* you *energize* the process by looking at your leadership skills and placing your attention on them. You *mobilize* by noticing or examining the current results you are getting from the people around you. You *internalize* by telling the truth about what is working and not working with your leadership ability. You will ultimately *realize* by taking an authentic action to make any necessary adjustments or enhancements. Be confident that life supports growth and rewards action. If you make the commitment to become *clear, confident,* and *capable* in developing an authentic mindset, your natural ability and delivery will unfold.

Leadership is not what you do, it is what others do because you are there. Moving from *selling* to *serving* will put you in your place of most potential. By being clear on who you are, confident in what you will do, and capable of aligning your intentions with actions, you become a first-rate version of yourself. People will be attracted to you, because you connect with them empathetically and contribute substantial value to their lives. They will be drawn to your vision, because they share similar values and qualities. Above all, you will empower people and help them stay in integrity with themselves.

What this can mean to you is to realize that by following your path and passion, you can have a profound impact on people's lives. The real benefit is that you will be content with what you have—because you have made peace with who you are.

My Authentic Vision: Correcting to 20/20

I coached my first workshop for the financial services industry in 1985. Al Granum, my general agent at the time, asked if I would be willing to talk about my process to a group of my peers, who by all standards were experienced and successful. These professionals viewed me as a promising associate and, for the most part, were curious about my methods and my fast start in our tough industry. One associate called me beforehand and said he heard I was putting on a "clinic" and was looking forward to attending. Hence, the vision of The Cassara Clinic was born.

The opportunity presented to me by Mr. Granum raised the question, "If the process I am using will be the process everyone else has to follow, will I change anything?" Three years into my career, I did not feel I had all the answers but was willing to share what I knew. The question made me look at my process and delivery system. I began to pay very close attention to what I was doing.

I completed the workshop and received very positive feedback from my peers. The clinic became a regular event in our agency, and soon other managers were requesting my workshop. By 1991, I was committing 40 days per year for clinics. The interesting thing was that the more days I spent teaching and coaching, the better my personal production became. I could *see* a direct correlation to working *on* my craft versus working *in* it. The more I practiced, so to speak, the more effective I became in my client relationships. I had the most productive years of my career from 1991 through 2000 while simultaneously coaching over 4,500 representatives.

In the year 2001, I was asked once again to share my process with a national audience of representatives. I spent three months looking, seeing, and telling the truth about my process and finetuning it. My authentic action was that I unveiled the second generation of the Client Creator process. More important were the feelings I had: I never felt more excited and alive in my professional life.

I declared publicly with the audience that I was in a transition in my life. After 20 years, I was pursuing my passion and changing my focus—at the age of 49. My peers asked me, "Can you make any money doing this?" My wife initially questioned, "Is this the right time?" and "Are we going to be okay financially?" The force of conformity was everywhere.

Many obstacles and challenges presented themselves. My marketing director relocated to California to pursue her dream. My administrative assistant and strategic partner both passed away within six months of each other. The events of September 11 created a whole new list of challenges. Confusion and chaos were the order of the day.

Many times, I could have said to hell with this and walked away. There are no accidents, and it always seemed that in those moments I would receive a phone call or letter from clients saying how much of a difference I had made in their lives. I felt I was being "called," and these challenges were testing my resolve and commitment. I was re-creating myself all over again, and it was uncomfortable.

Our personal power comes from the meaning we find in our lives. I knew that to delay and deny my vision was to deny who I was and how I could serve. I recognized the opportunity again when my friend, Alan, on his deathbed said, "You have to do this, Lou, the world needs you." His last blessing to me was another small miracle. He provided the right words at the right time.

I recognized the opportunity to serve others with my vision was, in fact, the way to provide the same results for myself. We teach what we seek to learn, and it was time to know something—not know about something.

My authentic vision is to be a leading resource of professional development for the financial services industry. To guide people to their greatness by bringing their life to their business to bring their business to life. To encourage others to do what they do best and do it to the best of their ability. To lead and serve others through my passion, dedication, and wisdom.

My friend, your greatness lies in the unknown. Your authentic vision provides the straight and narrow path. It will provide you with the mechanics to fulfill your destiny. You get there by going through your discomfort and re-creating yourself. As with all great endeavors, it takes courage to be your authentic self.

I will promise you this, you will feel alive—and what this world needs right now more than anything else is people who feel alive.

A *u t h e n t i c* **T** *r u t h s*

- Be clear your greatest power is to be willing.

- Be confident that life supports growth.

- Be capable of impacting the lives of others.

TAKING AUTHENTIC ACTION

EXERCISE

What will you continue to do? (What is working?) _____

_____

_____

_____

What will you stop doing? (What is not working?) _____

_____

_____

_____

_____

WHAT WILL YOU START DOING?

State one new intention _____

_____

_____

_____

_____

Engage one new action _____

_____

_____

_____

_____

Envision the result _____

_____

_____

_____

_____

FROM BELIEVING TO KNOWING

"Wisdom is knowing what to do next,
skill is knowing how to do it, and virtue is doing it."
DAVID STARR JORDAN

"A teacher effects eternity; he can never
tell where his influence stops."
HENRY ADAMS

BUILDING TO AN AUTHENTIC MINDSET

Be **clear** *your greatest power is to be willing.*

Be **confident** *that life supports growth.*

Be **capable** *of going into your discomfort to discover your greatness.*

One of the most important lessons I have ever learned is, *life is a process of creation.* We are creating the circumstances in our lives all the time. I believe we are divinely blessed when we have the experience of aligning our thoughts, words, and deeds to create the highest vision of ourselves.

Let me leave you with a story about courage and commitment—a story that should remind you that *the greatest gift you give to others is the example of your life working.*

My son, Anthony, was a freshman in high school when he announced to my wife and me one evening at dinner that he was going to try out for a part in the school play. We were impressed, given the fact that Anthony's school was known for its fine arts program with outstanding talent and great performances. He then went on to share that he would be trying out for a lead in the play, and this got my attention. He proceeded to say that the lead required him to sing and perform a solo. The play was *The King and I*, and his part was Prince Chulalonghorn. My wife and I encouraged him, and off he went to the tryout.

Without having any prior experience in theater, Anthony made the first cut. Two nights later he returned from the final audition with a big smile on his face and informed us that he got the part. We all congratulated him and let him know we could not wait to see his performance.

Two weeks before opening night, I was writing in my study when my daughter came in looking very worried and concerned and said, "Dad, you have to go upstairs and help Anthony. He is really having a tough time."

"What is the matter?" I asked, initially thinking that it probably was not that big of a deal. My daughter was concerned, firm, and to the point.

"He won't go to practice, and he is thinking of quitting the play. He will not talk to me. I really think you should go up there."

The people who know me well know I always put family ahead of business. I have lost opportunities by choosing family over work, but it is something I live by. I recently spoke to an audience and shared with them how the average person watches television for 33 hours per week and spends less than five minutes per day in intimate conversation. It was time to walk my talk. I dropped what I was doing and headed upstairs.

The door to Anthony's room was partially open, and as I knocked I could see him sitting on his bed, his face in his hands, almost in a fetal position. As I entered his room, I said to myself, *God, please give me the right thing to say to this boy at this time.* I could see he was in great pain, and my thoughts flashed back to when I was a kid and had my own painful times. I knew intuitively this would be no ordinary father-son chat. What I said to him at this point was going to make or break his self-esteem.

I walked in and sat on his bed and said, "Anthony, what is the matter son?"

He looked up at me and with panic in his voice said, "Dad, I just can't do this."

I reached out and put my hand on his shoulder and said, "Anthony, look at me son."

He took his hands away from his face, and I could see that he had been crying. I said, "Anthony, you are my son. I am going to love you no matter what you decide to do. It does not matter to me one way or another if you go through with this play or not. I *would* like to ask you a question, if it is okay."

"Sure," he nodded.

"Think about when you decided to go for the lead role. Why did you choose to get involved? What were you looking to accomplish?"

He thought for a few seconds and said, "I wanted to see how I could speak in front of an audience. I wanted to see if I could sing."

"Anthony," I said, "do you remember the time after I spoke in front of an audience that you came up and asked me what that was like?"

He nodded.

"Do you remember what I shared with you after that experience—that life rewards action and not intention?"

He nodded again.

"Well, *most opportunities come in our lives at what appear to be inappropriate times.* We see them as distractions and do not follow through on them. I can relate to what you are feeling, because the first time I spoke in front of an audience I felt the same way. But here is what is important: You would not have had this opportunity presented to you if you were not ready to experience it and learn something very special by doing it. Does that make any sense to you?"

Another nod.

"Here is something else you need to think about: You made an agreement with your peers and your drama coach to participate in this play. If you choose to walk away, make that choice understanding that you are going to disappoint a lot of people. They most likely are going to talk about you and give you a hard time. More important, how are you going to personally feel about yourself? So, does your decision to leave make you feel comfortable or uncomfortable?"

"Uncomfortable," he said, "very uncomfortable."

"Can I share something else with you? In my 48 years of life, I have learned that *delay is the worst form of denial.* Whenever I denied myself the opportunity of experiencing the type of discomfort you are feeling right now—when I told myself I could not do something because I was anxious or uncomfortable trying something new—that is when I really felt the most pain. Until I got in front of an audience and made my first speech, I did not know what that discomfort meant. Am I making any sense?"

"Yeah," he said, "I could see that, Dad."

"The most important lesson I learned through all of that, Anthony, is that *if I did not go within myself at the time of my discomfort, I almost always came away without learning something about myself.* Then I thought about the times that I dealt with my discomfort and went through it—like going away to college, buying my first home, getting married to your mother—and I remembered that on the other side was always a positive result, something better than before. That is what your feeling is trying to tell you. Why don't you go through it right now? Why don't you try it in front of all of us? If you can sing in front of your mom, me, and your sisters, you can do it anywhere."

Before he even answered, I jumped up, ran to the door, and called the family to his room. I got the soundtrack CD and put it in his player. Everyone sat around on the floor as Anthony sang to the music. He sang a little lethargically the first time, but we all gave him an ovation and encouraged him to try it again. He sang it about six more times, each time getting better and stronger than the one before. After his last performance, we all stood up and gave him a standing ovation.

He then made the choice to go to practice.

Two weeks later my wife and I sat packed into a darkened theater on opening night. I had butterflies in my stomach like the ones I get before I speak, and my wife was nothing short of a nervous wreck. (To this day, I tease her that I still have the nail marks in my arm where she dug into me while she was waiting for the play to begin.) After what seemed like an eternity, the houselights dimmed, the band struck up the theme to *The King and I,* and the stage was set. After several minutes in Act One, Anthony approached the stage. He walked to the edge of the stage with the strut of a prince, faced the audience, and delivered his first set of lines flawlessly.

My wife and I looked at each other and simultaneously exhaled a temporary sigh of relief as we waited for his upcoming solo. After about ten minutes, the new scene was set and the stage went dark, except for the spotlight that followed Anthony out to center stage. The band started, and the music filled the hall. Anthony, with great presence, turned, faced the audience, and sang.

He sang.

As the song came to an end, I could see the look of anxiety on his face change to relief and then change again to a huge smile when the audience cheered and clapped. At that very moment, I knew I had just witnessed a great life experience for my son.

At the close of the play, the cast was reintroduced with the lead actors coming out last. As Anthony came out for his curtain call, the audience jumped to its feet and gave him a standing ovation. Anthony beamed, as his mother and I swelled with emotion. Right before my eyes, I watched this young man transform from *believing* he could do it to *knowing* he could do it. He had learned a great life lesson, that *your life begins at the end of your comfort zone— by going into his discomfort and pain, he discovered himself and his greatness.*

After the play, all his friends rushed up to him and congratulated him. Girls were giving him bouquets of flowers and asking him to take photos with them. His self-esteem and confidence were sky-high.

On the ride home, Anthony kept thanking his mother and me for our support in helping him get through this experience. As I watched him talk to his sisters through my rearview mirror, I connected with my own profile. My mind flashed back to when I was 15 years old, and I imagined how my father would have handled this situation.

A smile came to my face as I thought about my answer. I glanced in my rearview mirror again, surrounded by the love of my family, and gave myself a wink. Truthfully, I knew in my heart that I did the very best I could and did it to the best of my ability.

Authentic **T**ruths

- Delay is the worst form of denial.

- Go within or go without.

- Your life begins at the end of your comfort zone.

EXCELLENCE

Tentative efforts lead to tentative outcomes. Therefore, give yourself fully to your endeavors. Decide to construct your character through excellent actions and determine to pay the price of a worthy goal. The trials you encounter will introduce you to your strengths. Remain steadfast . . . and one day you will build something that endures: something worthy of your potential.

EPICTETUS
ROMAN TEACHER AND PHILOSOPHER
AD 55–135

ANYWAY

People are often unreasonable, illogical and self-centered.
Forgive them anyway.
If you are kind, people may accuse you of selfish, ulterior motives.
Be kind anyway.
If you are successful, you will win some false friends and some true enemies.
Succeed anyway.
If you are honest and frank, people may cheat you.
Be honest and frank anyway.
What you spend years building someone could destroy overnight.
Build anyway.
If you find serenity and happiness, they may be jealous.
Be happy anyway.
The good you do today people will often forget tomorrow.
Do good anyway.
Give the world the best you have, and it may never be enough.
Give the world the best you've got anyway.
You see, in the final analysis, it is between you and God.
It was never between you and them anyway.

MOTHER TERESA HUNG A COPY OF THIS POEM ON A WALL
OF THE ORPHANAGE SHE FOUNDED IN CALCUTTA.
ITS SOURCE IS UNKNOWN.

authentic mindset Being a first-rate version of yourself and not a second-rate version of someone else

behavior Having the experience of who you are being

capability The result of combining your knowledge, talents, and skills to organize ideas and align intentions with actions

character Doing the right thing when no one is looking

choice A decision one makes to either avoid or create a particular outcome

clarity To be certain, open, and direct about something

client Someone who thinks of you first, last, and always for your product or service

compassion Understanding that people are doing the best they can with what they know

competition Creates a new mindset that more is possible and brings out the best in you

confidence The ability to think clearly, communicate effectively, and take authentic action.

dominant emotional response The number-one emotional reason that causes a person to act

emotion A thought with a feeling attached

essence of attraction Paying attention to what is going on inside of you at any given time

essence of commitment To get a commitment, one must make a commitment.

essence of connection To understand and activate the deep emotions in others

essence of vision Publicly stating and acting on your intentions are the highest form of visioning.

experiences All that is perceived, remembered, and understood

friend A person who will always tell you the truth

goals A compelling reason that projects your intentions into actions; a promise that you make to yourself

happy To be content with who you are

Integrity Quotient The ability to recognize the difference between the truth you know and the truth you live

intention A direction, aim, or purpose that comes from within you; the energy behind your goals

knowledge What you are aware of; consists of facts and lessons learned

law of attraction You will attract the very people and circumstances you need at any given time.

law of intention Every intention carries within itself the mechanics for its own fulfillment.

law of reciprocity What you take out of a relationship is in proportion to what you put into it.

pain A crisis, concern, dissatisfaction, disappointment, frustration, or fear

professional Someone who performs at their best, when they feel like it the least

relationships The primary teacher to help you remember and create who you are

result A plan with the necessary tasks that need be done; the outcome produced when actions are aligned with intentions

sale The ability to influence the outcome of a situation

significant Sustaining, long term, and reciprocal

skills The steps of an activity; the how-tos of a role

success The expansion of happiness you enjoy by acting on a truth that you know

talent A recurring pattern of thought, feeling, or behavior that can be productively applied

values The beliefs and standards that guide our intentions and actions

whole To align your thoughts, words, and deeds

yourself To express your unique abilities

Albion, Mark. *Making a Life, Making a Living: Reclaiming Your Purpose and Passion in Business and in Life.* New York: Warner Books, 2000.

Alcoholics Anonymous. *Twelve Steps and Twelve Traditions.* New York: Alcoholics Anonymous World Services, 2002.

Allen, James. *As a Man Thinketh.* Mechanicsburg, Pa.: Executive Books, 2001.

Anthony, Mitch. *Selling with Emotional Intelligence: Five Skills for Building Stronger Client Relationships.* Chicago: Dearborn Trade, 2003.

Autry, James A. *Love and Profit: The Art of Caring Leadership.* New York: Avon Books, 1991.

Beckwith, Harry. *Selling the Invisible: A Field Guide to Modern Marketing.* New York: Warner Books, 1997.

Buckingham, Marcus, and Donald O. Clifton. *Now Discover Your Strengths.* New York: The Free Press, 2001.

Buford, Bob. *Half Time: Changing Your Game Plan from Success to Significance.* Grand Rapids, Mich.: Zondervan, 1994.

Carnegie, Dale. *How to Win Friends and Influence People.* New York: Pocket Books, 1936.

Cassara, Lou. *The Client Creator Process: The Three Drivers to Attract, Connect and Commit to Significant Client Relationships.* Oak Brook, Ill.: Cassara Clinic, 2002.

A Course in Miracles. New York: Penguin Group, 1996.

Covey, Stephen R. *The Seven Habits of Highly Effective People.* New York: Simon and Schuster, 1989.

Decker, Bert. *You've Got to Be Believed to Be Heard.* New York: St. Martin's Press, 1992.

Dyer, Wayne W. *There's a Spiritual Solution to Every Problem.* New York: Harper Collins, 2001.

Eldredge, John. *Wild at Heart: Discovering the Secret of a Man's Soul.* Nashville, Tenn.: Thomas Nelson, 2001.

Granum, Alfred. *The Science, the Art of Building a Life Insurance Clientele.* Cincinnati, Ohio: The National Underwriter Company, 1975.

Hawkins, David R. *Power versus Force: The Hidden Determinants of Human Behavior.* Carlsbad, Calif.: Hay House, 2002.

Hay, Louise L. *You Can Heal Your Life.* Carlsbad, Calif.: Hay House, 1994.

Hill, Napoleon. *Think and Grow Rich.* Los Angeles: Renaissance Books, 1960.

Kolbe, Kathy. *Pure Instinct: Business' Untapped Resource.* New York: Times Books, 1993.

Levoy, Gregg. *Callings: Finding and Following an Authentic Life.* New York: Three Rivers Press, 1997.

McNally, David. *Even Eagles Need a Push: Learning to Soar in a Changing World.* New York: Dell Trade Paperback, 1990.

McNair, Colonel Nimrod. *Absolute Ethics: A Proven System for True Profitability.* Tucker, Ga.: Executive Leadership Foundation, 1987.

———. *Mega Values: Ten Global Principles for Business and Professional Success Written in Stone.* Tucker, Ga.: Executive Leadership Foundation, 1996.

Mapes, James J. *Quantum Leap Thinking.* Los Angeles: Dove Audio, 1996.

Nemeth, Maria. *The Energy of Money: A Spiritual Guide to Financial and Personal Fulfillment.* New York: Ballantine, 1999.

Ruiz, Don Miguel. *The Four Agreements.* San Rafael, Calif.: Amber-Allen Publishing, 1997.

Secretan, Lance. *Inspirational Leadership: Destiny, Calling and Cause.* Toronto, Canada: The Secretan Centre, 1999.

Staub, Robert E. II. *The Acts of Courage: Bold Leadership for a Whole Hearted Life.* Provo, Utah: Executive Excellence Publishing, 1999.

Sullivan, Dan. *The Great Crossover: Personal Confidence in the Age of the Microchip.* Toronto, Canada: The Strategic Coach, 1994.

Walsch, Neale Donald. *Conversations with God: An Uncommon Dialogue.* New York: Putnam, 1996.

West, Scott, and Mitch Anthony. *Storyselling for Financial Advisors: How Top Producers Sell.* Chicago: Dearborn Trade, 2000.

THE CLIENT CREATOR™ PROCESS

The Client Creator™ Process is a professional development program designed to help participants create significant relationships using powerful principles and strategies that challenge them to improve their communication, develop their process and enhance their presentation.

DEVELOP YOUR SKILLS AND CREATE RESULTS

- **Develop your Personal Value Statement™**

  Communicate what you do clearly, effectively and with purpose in both business and personal settings. Articulate the benefits of working with you, to prospects and peers, dramatically increasing their interest in you and your process.

- **Build credibility**

  Develop your own unique process. Understand that this is your true product, not your commodity or your service.

- **Create significant relationships**

  Build personal and professional relationships that are reciprocal and in which you are utilized, enhanced, appreciated, rewarded and referred.

- **Develop your growth strategy**

  Evaluate the motivation behind your career and consciously align your intentions with your actions and behavior.

- **Bring your business to life!**

  Empower yourself to achieve your vision by making the changes necessary to move to the next level of productivity. Focus on having a life rather than on just making a living.

FOR MORE INFORMATION

Visit us online at www.cassaraclinic.com, or call us at 888.848.6818.